Mystery of God

faith first

Legacy Edition

RCL Benziger®

Cincinnati, Ohio

This book reflects the new revision of the

ROMAN MISSAL
THIRD EDITION

"The Ad Hoc Committee to Oversee the Use of the Catechism, United States Conference of Catholic Bishops, has found this catechetical series, copyright 2006, to be in conformity with the *Catechism of the Catholic Church*."

NIHIL OBSTAT
Reverend Robert M. Coerver
Censor Librorum

IMPRIMATUR
† Most Rev. Charles V. Grahmann
Bishop of Dallas
September 1, 2004

The Nihil Obstat and Imprimatur are official declarations that the material reviewed is free of doctrinal or moral error. No implication is contained therein that those granting the Nihil Obstat and Imprimatur agree with the contents, opinions, or statements expressed.

Send all inquiries to:
RCL Benziger
8805 Governor's Hill Drive
Suite 400
Cincinnati, Ohio 45249

Toll Free   877-275-4725
Fax   800-688-8356

Visit us at **www.RCLBenziger.com**
             www.FaithFirst.com

Printed in the United States of America

20487   ISBN 978-0-7829-1069-8 (Student Book)
20488   ISBN 978-0-7829-1081-0 (Catechist Guide)
20527   ISBN 978-0-7829-1112-1 (Teacher Guide)

7th printing.
Manufactured for RCL Benziger in Cincinnati, OH, USA.
March 2012.

ACKNOWLEDGMENTS

Scripture excerpts are taken or adapted from the *New American Bible with Revised New Testament and Psalms* Copyright © 1991, 1986, 1970, Confraternity of Christian Doctrine, Washington, DC. Used with permission. All rights reserved. No part of the *New American Bible* may be reproduced by any means without the permission of the copyright owner.

Excerpts are taken or adapted from the English translation of the *Roman Missal* © 2010, International Committee on English in the Liturgy, Inc. (ICEL); excerpts from *A Book of Prayers* © 1982, ICEL; *Catholic Household Blessings and Prayers* (revised edition) © 2007, United States Conference of Catholic Bishops, Washington, D.C. All rights reserved.

Faith First Legacy Edition Development Team

Developing a religion program requires the gifts and talents of many individuals working together as a team. RCL Benziger is proud to acknowledge the contributions of these dedicated people.

Program Theology Consultants
Reverend Louis J. Cameli, S.T.D.
Reverend Robert D. Duggan, S.T.D.

Advisory Board
Judith Deckers, M.Ed.
Elaine McCarron, SCN, M.Div.
Marina Herrera, Ph.D.
Reverend Frank McNulty, S.T.D.
Reverend Ronald J. Nuzzi, Ph.D.

National Catechetical Advisor
Jacquie Jambor

Catechetical Specialist
Jo Rotunno

Contributing Writers
Student Book and Catechist Guide
Christina DeCamp
Judith Deckers
Mary Beth Jambor
Eileen A. McGrath
Reverend Robert D. Duggan
Reverend Steven M. Lanza
Michele Norfleet

Art & Design Director
Lisa Brent

Electronic Page Makeup
Laura Fremder

Production Director
Jenna Nelson

Designers/Photo Research
Pat Bracken
Kristy O. Howard
Susan Smith

Project Editors
Patricia A. Classick
Steven M. Ellair
Ronald C. Lamping

Web Site Producers
Joseph Crisalli
Demere Henson

General Editor
Ed DeStefano

President/Publisher
Maryann Nead

Contents

Welcome to Faith First 5

Unit One The Revelation of God

Getting Ready 8

Chapter 1 We Believe 9

Faith concepts: The quest for God; natural knowledge of God; Saint Augustine of Hippo; Saint Albert the Great; faith and reason; divine Revelation; the gift of faith, faith seeking understanding, mysteries of faith, atheism, agnosticism, secularism, secular humanism
Scripture: Psalm 27:8, 1 Corinthians 13:12
Faith-living skills: Getting in touch with God
Prayer: Act of Faith

Chapter 2 The Word of God 19

Faith concepts: Inspiration of the Bible; the Canon of Sacred Scripture; oral tradition; literary genre in the Bible; the Covenant with Noah, with Abraham and Moses; the land of Abraham; promise of a new covenant; Sacred Tradition
Scripture: Acts of the Apostles 6:4; Genesis 9:8–10, 12–13; Deuteronomy 7:6–9; Jeremiah 11:4
Faith-living skills: Communication skills
Prayer: Praying the Scriptures

Chapter 3 The Man Born Blind: A Scripture Story . . 29

Faith concepts: The Fourth Gospel; Saint John the Apostle and Evangelist; Book of Signs; miracles; Jesus' healing the man born blind, faith in Jesus, initiation into the Catholic Church
Scripture: John 9:2–7, 30–31, 33–34, 35–38; John 20:30–31
Faith skills: Overcoming obstacles to seeing with eyes of faith
Prayer: Signing of the Senses

Chapter 4 The Mystery of Creation 39

Faith concepts: Attributes of God: Almighty, Creator, One, Eternal, Truth, All-Present, Love; the biblical accounts of creation of humans, spiritual soul; original justice, original sin; new creation, Jesus the new Adam; Saint Teresa of Avila
Scripture: Genesis 1:26, 27, 31; 2:7; Deuteronomy 6:4–5; 2 Samuel 7:28; Isaiah 54:10; Romans 1:20; Colossians 1:15–16; 1 John 4:8
Faith-living skills: Building healthy relationships
Prayer: Praise God

Chapter 5 God: Father, Son, and Holy Spirit 49

Faith concepts: The mystery of God; the Holy Trinity; Saint Athanasius and the First Council of Nicea; nature and person; the work of the Trinity, attribution and the divine missions: creation, salvation, and sanctification; the Christian family
Scripture: Genesis 1:2; John 1:1–8, 14:10, 16–17, 26
Faith-living skills: Balancing relationships within the family
Prayer: Apostles' Creed

Unit One Review 59

Unit Two The Gift of Salvation

Getting Ready 62

Chapter 6 Jesus Christ, the Son of God 63

Faith concepts: Blessed Mary, Ever-Virgin; Immaculate Conception; Mary, Mother of God; the Incarnation: Jesus, true God and true man; Infancy Narratives; public ministry of Jesus; ecumenical councils of the Church; symbols for Jesus Christ
Scripture: Galatians 4:4; John 1:1, 14; Luke 4:18–19; Philippians 2:11
Faith-living skills: Respecting and accepting differences
Prayer: Benedictus

Chapter 7 The Transfiguration of Jesus: A Scripture Story 73

Faith concepts: Mountains in Sacred Scripture; the Jewish feast of Tabernacles; the Transfiguration, Moses and the prophet Elijah, Jesus the fulfillment of the Law and Prophets, Jesus the suffering Messiah; Blessed Mother Teresa of Calcutta
Scripture: Psalm 89:9, 13; Matthew 16:15, 16; 17:2–13
Faith-living skills: Seeing with eyes of faith
Prayer: The Gloria

Chapter 8 The Suffering Servant: A Scripture Story . . 83

Faith concepts: Isaiah the Prophet; the Book of the Prophet Isaiah: the servant songs, the Servant of YHWH, the suffering Servant; the major and minor prophets; Jesus the sinless, suffering Servant; the suffering Church; Archbishop Helder Camara
Scripture: Hebrews 5:8–9; Isaiah 52:13–15; 53:1–2; 53:3, 7–8, 11–12; Matthew 26:28
Faith-living skills: Dealing with loss
Prayer: Veneration of the Cross

Chapter 9 Jesus' Passion and Death 93

Faith concepts: The origin and problem of evil: original justice, original sin; Jesus the New Adam; Jesus' death and descent to the dead; Stations of the Cross
Scripture: Genesis 2:17, John 19:30, 1 Peter 4:6
Faith-living skills: Moving from sadness to hope
Prayer: Litany of the Holy Name of Jesus

Chapter 10 Jesus' Resurrection and Ascension 103

Faith concepts: The Resurrection; the Ascension; life after death: particular judgment, Last Judgment, heaven, purgatory, hell; Saint Philip Neri
Scripture: Acts of the Apostles 1:9–11, John 11:25–26, 1 Corinthians 15:3–6, Hebrews 9:24
Faith-living skills: Persevering in living the Gospel
Prayer: Christ, Our Hope

Chapter 11 A Resurrection Story: A Scripture Story 113

Faith concepts: Resurrection stories: pattern, audience, setting, faith testimonies; Saint Thomas the Apostle; appearance of Risen Jesus at Sea of Tiberias; symbolism of the number 7, light and darkness, the breaking of Bread; stained-glass windows
Scripture: John 21:12, Matthew 28:8–17, Mark 16:9–18, Luke 24:1–49, John 20:11–31, John 21:1–23
Faith-living skills: Faith sharing
Prayer: The Lord Is Risen: A Profession of Faith

Chapter 12 The Holy Spirit, the Sanctifier 123

Faith concepts: The Holy Spirit in the Old Covenant, in the Gospels, in the work of Christ, in the life of the Church; the Advocate; charisms and the Gifts of the Holy Spirit; Christian art
Scripture: Ezekiel 37:1–3, 11, 12, 14; Matthew 10:20; Luke 11:13; John 3:5; Acts of the Apostles 2:2–4; 1 Corinthians 3:16; 2 Corinthians 6:16
Faith-living skills: Living the Gifts of the Holy Spirit
Prayer: Prayer to the Holy Spirit

Unit Two Review 133

Catholic Prayers and Practices 135

Glossary 147

Index 150

Credits 152

Welcome to Faith First

Welcome to **Faith First: The Mystery of God.** God's Revelation to us is the source of our faith and the source of many of our questions about life. This book invites you to explore your personal faith and the faith of the Church to which you belong. You will gain deeper insight into the word God has revealed in Sacred Scripture and in the Sacred Tradition of the Catholic Church. You will begin to understand more clearly the significance of God's Revelation to the Hebrew people and the fullness of that Revelation that takes place in the life, Passion, death, Resurrection, and Ascension of Jesus Christ.

In every chapter you will be asked to make a faith response to what you are learning. The knowledge you gain about the mystery of God will only bear fruit if you allow it to make a difference in your life. So, let's get started and explore more deeply the greatest mystery of all—the mystery of God.

The Mystery of God

Beginning Reflections

There is one God who is Father, Son, and Holy Spirit. This doctrine of the Holy Trinity is the central mystery of our faith. In the weeks ahead you will come to know more about the three persons of the Holy Trinity and how God has revealed himself to his people through Sacred Scripture and the Sacred Tradition of the Church.

Every day of your life God is calling you to come to know him better. You accepted this call at your Baptism. Consider the following reflections. Jot down your initial responses. This reflection time will help you open the doors of your mind and heart to experience more deeply the mystery of a loving, caring God.

Approach the study of God with wonder and awe. God is so much greater than all our ideas of him.

I am inspired to look at God with wonder and awe when

_____

_____

_____ .

Remember that through the words of Scripture God is revealing himself to you. There is always more we can learn about the mystery of God.

One thing I have learned about the mystery of God through the words of Scripture is

_____

_____

_____ .

Deepen your prayer life. After you have finished each class session, and at the end of each day, reflect on what you have learned. Rest for a moment in the mystery of God's love.

Prayer affects my relationship with God by

_____

_____

_____ .

Participate as fully as possible in each class session. The discussions and activities are designed to help you apply to your life what you are learning about your faith.

The effort I put into learning more about the mystery of God could result in

_____

_____ .

Accept the challenge to live as a child of God, a follower of Christ. Believe that God is always present with you. Reach out to others. Be a sign of God's love in the world.

I can choose to be a sign of God's love in the world. One specific way I can do this is by

_____

_____

UNIT ONE
The Revelation of God

What can we know about God?

Getting Ready

The Holy Trinity

What do you already know about the Holy Trinity?

_____

_____

_____

_____

_____

_____

_____

_____

_____

Questions I Have

What questions about God do you hope these chapters will answer?

_____

_____

_____

_____

_____

A Scripture Story

Jesus healing the man born blind

What does the Gospel story tell you about Jesus?

Faith Vocabulary

Put an X next to the faith vocabulary terms that you know. Put a ? next to the faith vocabulary terms that you need to know more about.

_____ divine Revelation

_____ faith

_____ Sacred Scripture

_____ Sacred Tradition

_____ Evangelists

_____ miracle

_____ divine Providence

_____ soul

_____ omnipresence

_____ mystery

_____ dogma

_____ Holy Trinity

We Believe

FAITH FOCUS

How do both faith and reason help us come to know God?

FAITH VOCABULARY

divine Revelation

faith

mystery

What experiences make you the happiest?

Every person has an unquenchable thirst for happiness. Some people search to satisfy that thirst by acquiring power or prestige or popularity or possessions. Experience shows that getting a little power can easily lead to seeking more power; becoming popular creates the need to be more popular. And so it goes. More . . . more . . . and more. . . . It seems that "more" is never quite enough. The more we get, the more we seem to need—or want.

We watch the growth of technology in amazement. Still, with all the discoveries that fill our hearts with adventure and excitement, we know that our discovery of the wonder of the world has really just begun!

How does your discovery of the wonder of creation help you come to know God?

"Come," says my heart, "seek God's face"; / your face, LORD, do I seek!

PSALM 27:8

Our Search for Happiness

The Quest for God

Another search has filled the lives of all people since our beginning. It is the search for God.

The religions of people who have lived or who are living in Oceania, Asia, Europe, Africa, and the Americas remind us that human history itself can be told as the story of the search of the human heart and mind for God.

We are religious by our very nature. God puts into the very core of every person a longing for God. God made us with a desire for him.

One of the most famous quotes in all of the world's religious writings appears in *Confessions*, an autobiography by Saint Augustine of Hippo (A.D. 354–430).

Speaking to God, Augustine says:

> You have made us for yourself, and our heart is restless until it rests in you.

When we listen to the voice of our conscience, we can come to know with certainty that God exists. He is the "more" we are always searching for. God is the cause and the end of everything. He is the Creator and Lord.

What are some of the ways you show that your relationship with God brings you happiness?

Coming to Know God

We have been created to live in friendship and communion with God. We become fully human only when we recognize that God created us and we find our happiness in him.

We can come to know God through his creation. The beauty, greatness, and symmetry of the universe point to God who made all things and keeps them in existence. The magnificence of the universe is a reflection of the awesome goodness and power of God. The more science enables us to discover the symmetry, or order, in nature, the more our belief in the existence of God is strengthened.

FAITH CONNECTION

Describe a photograph that you would choose to illustrate the goodness and power of God.

_____

_____

_____

The Search for Truth

The Church is a community of believers. We are a people of faith. We are a community of people who stand in awe and wonder at the ability of the human mind to discover God in the secrets of creation and in the order of the universe.

Throughout history Christians have taken their place among the great scientists of the world. Saint Albert the Great (ca.1206–1280) was one of the world's great scientists.

Albert was so respected that he has come to be known as Albertus Magnus, or Albert the Great.

Albert was also a person of faith. He was convinced that our human minds were limited in what they could know on their own. He taught that we come to know things in different ways. Each type of knowledge has its own way of investigating or researching the truth. Albert argued that we can never "prove" or "disprove" the truths of our faith by our human minds. Otherwise they would be proven, not believed!

Christians believe there can be no "real" contradiction between the "truths" that we learn through science and other forms of human learning and the "truths" that we believe in faith. This is another way of saying that faith and reason can never really contradict each other. We make such a statement because God is the source of all truth.

Sometimes there may seem to be differences between what we know by faith and what we learn through science and human reason. We may not be able to explain these differences—at the moment. This happens because our knowledge and understanding of the truth that we have come to by science and reason alone has its limits. There will always be more to know and understand not only about God but also about ourselves and the wonders of the created universe.

When have you been willing to believe something you didn't really understand because a parent or person you respect said it was true?

Divine Revelation

In addition to these human ways of coming to know God, we come to know God in another way. God has made known, or revealed, things about himself that we can never come to know on our own. He has revealed these hidden mysteries of who he is so that we can get to know and believe in him better. We call this **divine Revelation.**

God's revelation of himself is God's free gift of making himself known to us and giving himself to us by gradually communicating his own mystery in deeds and words. It is God inviting us to know him, hope in him, and love him above all else.

God invites us to accept in **faith** what he has revealed. First, faith is a supernatural gift of God. God invites us and gives us the power to open our mind, our will, our whole being to him. Faith is the virtue, or power, that enables us to respond to God and to believe the truths he has revealed because of his own authority. It gives us the power to know God, seek him above all things, and live with him forever.

Second, faith is our free, conscious human response to God, who is all-good and all-loving. Faith is our personal, deliberate commitment to God. It is the free assent of our intellect and will to God's self-revelation. We accept the full truth of God's revelation because of who God is and because God has given us his word.

What is the connection between revelation and faith?

Faith Seeks Understanding

Sometimes people have questions and even serious difficulties about their faith in God and in what he has revealed. When people of faith have these questions and difficulties, they may worry that their faith may be weak—or even absent.

To seek a deeper understanding of the truth, especially God's revealed truth, is part of our human nature. This human process of seeking a deeper understanding of divine Revelation is the reason religion teachers and catechists help students work at understanding the teachings of the Catholic Church and to seek answers to the questions about their faith. Seeking a better understanding of our faith helps us grow more deeply as people of faith.

No matter how deep our faith, no matter how much we think we understand our faith and can explain it to others, God always remains a **mystery.** He is a mystery whom humans can never fully understand and our words can never completely explain. With faith, we are given the eyes to see a glimpse of eternal Truth, who is God. Paul the Apostle wrote this about Revelation and the gift of faith:

At present we see indistinctly, as in a mirror, but then face to face.

1 CORINTHIANS 13:12

FAITH CONNECTION

Design a card that could be handed out to others. On the card write a list of ways that a person can come to a deeper understanding of God.

_____

_____

_____

OUR CHURCH
MAKES A DIFFERENCE

The Learning Church and the Teaching Church

Christians have always devoted themselves to studying and sharing with others what they have come to know about God and his Revelation to us. Catholic educators have always sought to teach as Jesus, who was honored as Rabbi, or Teacher, taught.

Catholic Elementary and High School Education

Catholic education has a long history in the United States of America. Missionaries traveled with the explorers and taught the Gospel to the native inhabitants of the New World. In 1662 the Jesuits opened a school in New York City, which they were forced to close in 1689. In 1782 the first parochial school was founded at St. Mary's Church in Philadelphia, Pennsylvania.

The growth of Catholic elementary education in the United States increased in the early 1800s under the leadership of Catholic educators like Mother Elizabeth Bayley Seton. Mother Seton was named a saint of the Church in 1975. She was the first native-born American to be named a saint and is honored as a patron saint of Catholic schools.

Today parish religious education programs, parish schools, and Catholic high schools continue to help us learn and live our faith. In the United States of America more than 19,000 parishes serve over 4,000,000 elementary and high school students. More than 6,500 Catholic elementary schools serve nearly 1,900,000 students, and more than 750,000 students are enrolled in more than 1,300 Catholic high schools.

Catholic Colleges and Universities

The story of Catholic colleges and universities in the United States of America began with Georgetown College (Georgetown University in Washington, D.C.), which was founded in 1789 and opened for classes in 1791. Today, there are about 700,000 students enrolled in more than 200 Catholic colleges and universities.

Who helps you learn about God and God's wonderful creation? How do they help you understand and live your faith?

WHAT DIFFERENCE
Does Faith Make in My Life?

Getting in Touch with God

For many years you have been learning about the Catholic faith and discovering the difference it makes for your life. One thing your parents and teachers and catechists have been emphasizing is that your search for God is the same as your search for real happiness.

How can you go about searching for and discovering real happiness? Just as you hang out with your friends and talk and listen and enjoy their friendship, you also need to spend time with God. Here are some skills you can work on to do just that.

Pray

The very first thing to do is just be still and be with God. Prayer is communicating with God. Focus on God's presence with you. Listen first, and then talk things over with God.

What are some things you would like to talk over with God? How does sharing these things with God help you grow in your relationship with him?

_____

_____

_____

Read God's Word

Scripture is God's own word to us. Read the Bible with a listening ear. You will be surprised how much God tells you about happiness.

What is your favorite Scripture story? How does it help you grow in your relationship with God?

_____

_____

_____

See God in Others

God dwells in each of us. We are temples of the Holy Spirit. God speaks to you through others and your relationship with them. He speaks to you through the daily events of your life.

Who are the people who help you grow in your relationship with God?

_____

_____

Reflect on Creation

The goodness of creation is a reflection of God, the Creator, and his love. A beautiful sunset, a majestic ocean, even the playfulness of a pet can help you discover God's love for you. All are signs of God—the source of the happiness that creation brings us.

Think about creation. How does it help you discover God's love for you?

_____

_____

_____

Faith Decision

- In a small group discuss ways you get in touch with God.

- Talk about ways you think God gets in touch with you.

This week I will be more conscious of how God is calling me to know him better. To do this I will

_____

_____

_____.

PRAY and REVIEW

Act of Faith

Group 1:
O my God,
we firmly believe
that you are one God
    in three divine Persons,
    Father, Son, and Holy Spirit.

Group 2:
We believe
that your divine Son
    became man
and died for our sins,
and that he will come again
to judge the living and the dead.

Group 3:
We believe
these and all the truths
that the Catholic Church teaches
because you revealed them,
who can neither deceive
nor be deceived.

All:
Amen.

FAITH VOCABULARY

Define each of these faith terms:

1. divine Revelation   2. faith
3. mystery

MAIN IDEAS

Choose either (a) or (b) from each set of items. Write a brief paragraph to answer each of your choices.

1. (a) How is our search for happiness similar to our search for God?

   (b) Describe how we can come to know God through creation.

2. (a) Describe faith as both a gift and a response.

   (b) Explain why God, even after he reveals himself, is always a mystery.

CRITICAL THINKING

Using what you have learned in this chapter, explain this statement:
There can be no real contradiction between the truths of faith and the truths we learn from science.

FAMILY DISCUSSION

How can family members help one another grow in faith?

For more ideas on ways your family can live your faith, visit the "Faith First for Families" page at **www.FaithFirst.com**. Check out the Teen Center to discover this week's saint.

The Word of God

FAITH FOCUS

How do the different types of writings in the Bible help communicate God's word to us?

FAITH VOCABULARY

Bible	oral tradition
inspiration	literary genre
canon of Sacred Scripture	covenant

What expressions do you know that people use to get a point across?

You sometimes hear people say things that are not literally true; for example, "There must have been a million people at the game last night!" This expression is used to get the point across that there was a very large crowd at the game.

God first chose writers to write down his message to his people in words they knew and understood. These words were then translated into other languages.

Why is it important to understand there are many types of writing in the Bible?

"[W]e shall devote ourselves to prayer and to the ministry of the word."
ACTS OF THE APOSTLES 6:4

A book of the four Gospels in a well dressing

The Inspired Word of God

The **Bible,** or Sacred Scripture, is the collection of all the writings God has inspired human authors to write in his name. This means that God is the author of the Bible. We use the phrase **inspiration of the Bible** to name this belief of God's people. We believe that all the writings that make up the Bible have been written down by human authors with the help of the Holy Spirit.

The Canon of Sacred Scripture

The list of books that the Catholic Church teaches to be the inspired written word of God is called the **canon of Sacred Scripture.** There are forty-six books in the Old Testament and twenty-seven in the New Testament.

The Church teaches that God's message, or revelation, was first passed on to us by word of mouth. We call this **oral tradition.** Eventually this revelation was written down by God's people. The writing of the Old Testament began about a thousand years before the birth of Jesus Christ. The New Testament was completed about seventy years after the death-Resurrection of Jesus.

What are some stories that have been passed down in your family from earlier generations?

Jesus, the Center of the Bible

The Bible is one book. There is an unbreakable connection between the Old and the New Testaments. The Old Testament tells us about God's plan of saving love from creation up to the birth of Jesus. The four accounts of the Gospel are the heart, or center, of the Bible, because Jesus is their center. The writings of the New Testament pass on to us the Church's faith in who Jesus Christ is and in the meaning of his life, Passion, death, Resurrection, and glorious Ascension.

Describe the connection between the Old Testament and the New Testament.

Literary Genre

The vast collection of books that make up the Bible include many different styles of writing, or **literary genre**. These include history (Kings, Chronicles, the Acts of the Apostles), letters (Paul's epistles), and collections of sayings (Proverbs), poetry, and other forms of literary expression.

Just as our parents and teachers speak to us in many different ways, so do the writers of the Bible. They explain, warn, reprimand, comfort, praise, and so on. Each type of writing helps us, in its own way, understand what God is saying.

FAITH : CONNECTION

Look up these passages in a Bible. Name the genre of each passage.

1 Kings 5:9–14 _____

Proverbs 10:1–6 _____

Colossians 1:1–6 _____

The Story of the Covenant

Why would God inspire the people of God to write down his message? God wants everyone to know who he is and how much he wants all people to be happy with him now and forever.

In the Bible God tells us about the **Covenant** he made with humankind. A synonym for the word *covenant* is *testament*. The Old and the New Testaments tell the story of that covenant and its fulfillment in Jesus Christ, the New and Everlasting Covenant who is the Savior of the world.

God's Covenant with humankind began at creation. God entered an agreement with humankind through Adam and Eve who had been created to live in happiness with him. God ordered Adam not to eat from "the tree of knowledge of good and bad" (Genesis 2:17). You know what happened. The serpent's temptation was too much, and the first humans chose not to keep their part of the agreement.

God did not allow his plan of creation to be destroyed. God promised to send a descendant from Eve who would one day conquer the tempter, the devil. God's plan of loving and merciful salvation began.

The Covenant with Noah

Chapters 3 through 11 of the Book of Genesis tell us about the great evil of sin and its effects on people and God's creation. We read about Cain and Abel, Noah and the great flood, and the tower of Babel.

Covenant with Noah

We learn that when sin so divided people, God renewed the Covenant with Noah and all living things. In the Book of Genesis we read:

God said to Noah and to his sons with him: "See, I am now establishing my covenant with you and your descendants after you and with every living creature that was with you: . . . This is the sign that I am giving for all ages to come, of the covenant between me and you and every living creature with you: I set my bow in the clouds to serve as a sign of the covenant between me and the earth." Genesis 9:8–10, 12–13

God's covenant with Noah and all living things remains in force as long as the world lasts.

Describe the covenant God made with humankind through Noah.

Abraham and Moses

God next formed a covenant with Abraham. God promised that Abraham would become the father of a great nation (see Genesis 12:1–12). As the story of the Covenant unfolds, we learn that the Israelites are Abraham and Sarah's descendants.

God would later choose Moses to lead the Israelites, or Hebrews, out of slavery in Egypt. Through Moses God would reveal his Law to them and enter a covenant with them. He would be their God, and they would be his people (see Deuteronomy 7:6–9, Jeremiah 11:4).

Moses carrying the tablets containing the Ten Commandments

The Promise of a New Covenant

God's people eventually became a great nation. Under the leadership of King David and King Solomon, they became respected by their neighbors. However, perhaps because of their power and wealth, future kings and the people soon forgot their promises to God. God sent prophets, such as Ezekiel and Jeremiah, Amos and Hosea, to remind them of their covenant and to promise a new covenant (see Exodus 19–20).

We believe that all these events point to Jesus Christ. God has revealed himself fully by sending his own Son, Jesus, in whom he has established his covenant with humanity forever. Jesus Christ is the New Covenant.

Why do we say Jesus is the New Covenant?

Jesus, the New and Everlasting Covenant

Sacred Tradition

Part of the difficulty in understanding the Bible is the very fact that God chose human authors who used human words to tell us about himself. They wrote in their own languages truths that we might otherwise never know. So, if we know something about the writings and their language, we can better grasp the meaning of God's word.

Fortunately we belong to the Church whose understanding of these inspired writings can be relied upon. The Church is guided today by the same Holy Spirit that inspired the original writers of the Old Testament and the New Testament. With the guidance of the Holy Spirit, the teaching office of the Church has the responsibility of authentically interpreting the word of God. The pope and the bishops in communion with him are the center of this teaching office.

The passing on of our faith in Christ by the Church through the power of the Holy Spirit is called Sacred Tradition. The Church passes on its faith not just in the writings of the Bible but also in her prayer and in all of the many ways that the Church lives in faithfulness to the Lord. Through Scripture and Tradition God's revelation is passed on to us. Together they make up one source, or deposit of faith. From this source we continually draw our faith and are nourished at the banquet table of God's love.

FAITH CONNECTION

Work with a partner. Brainstorm as many ways as you can that the Catholic Church shows the world she is faithful to God's message.

_____

_____

_____

_____

OUR CHURCH
MAKES A DIFFERENCE

because we have just heard God speak to us. God's word has shared with us the deepest truth about life. God has spoken to us about how we can truly live in peace and happiness.

Praying the Scriptures

When we gather with the members of the Church to worship or when we read the Bible alone, God is always there for us. Faith in this truth is the reason we set time aside each day for reading the Bible. The evidence for this is that the Bible continues to be the most widely read book in the world.

How does your parish community show reverence for the word of God proclaimed at Mass? How can you make Scripture a more important part of your daily life?

The Table of God's Word

Sacred Scripture has always had a central place in Christian life. This is one of the reasons that the Catholic Church always includes the proclamation of Scripture as part of the liturgy, the official, public prayer of the Church. When the Church gathers for prayer, the Holy Spirit is present within us in a very powerful way.

Saint Augustine of Hippo taught that there are two tables from which we are fed at every Mass—the Table of the Word and the Table of the Eucharist. We believe that the Church draws its life from these two tables. This is why, at the end of the reading, we always say either "Thanks be to God" or "Praise to you, Lord Jesus Christ." We say this

WHAT DIFFERENCE
Does Faith Make in My Life?

Listening

Listening is crucial to communication. You may believe that communication is mostly talking, but talking is only half of it. Listening is the other half. If you do not listen to what is being said, there is no communication. Sometimes when someone speaks to you, your mind will begin to think its own thoughts—to think about what you want to say. You may not even hear the other person speaking.

Communication Skills

God wants to communicate with you. The Bible is the inspired word of God. When you read or listen to the Bible being read to you, you need to remember it is God's own word you are hearing.

You may believe that it is easy to communicate. You may think that if you just speak words clearly, you will be heard and understood. But to really communicate you need to develop certain skills.

Clarification

Clarification helps you understand what the other person is really saying. This skill is needed to understand what is really being said. For example, in the Old and the New Testaments, the writers used letters, poems, histories, and other different ways to make God's message very clear. Clarifying the type of writing you are reading is very important to understanding God's message. The same is true in your communication with family members, friends, and others.

Actions

Would it surprise you to know that experts say that only about 7 percent of communication has to do with words? Most of your communication, 93 percent, has to do with your actions—your facial expressions and tone of voice. For example, you might tell someone, "I like you; you're my friend," but your mean and hurtful actions might be communicating different messages. Remember that you show your love for God and others in both words and actions.

Faith· Decision

- Form a group of three that includes a speaker, a listener, and an observer. The speaker begins a conversation. The listener listens attentively and responds. The observer sits or stands behind the speaker and the listener and observes, saying nothing.

- When the conversation is finished, the observer shares what he or she perceived by answering these questions: How well did the one student really listen as the other one spoke? How clear was the exchange back and forth? What actions (tone, facial expressions, and so on) helped to make their message understood?

- If time permits, have the members of the triad switch roles.

This week I will try to communicate better with God by

_____

_____ .

PRAY and REVIEW

Praying the Scriptures

The Church has the tradition of praying the Scriptures. This practice is known as lectio divina, or divine reading. We use this form of praying to come to know God better, to listen to him speak in our hearts, and to love and serve him more.

Take the time to pray the Scriptures. Use these simple steps:

1. Choose a quiet place. Quiet your mind and relax. Remember God is with you.

2. Pray to the Holy Spirit. Ask the Spirit who dwells within you to open your mind and heart to God.

3. Open your Bible. Choose a Gospel reading. Picture yourself with Jesus.

4. Prayerfully read the Scripture. Listen attentively. God is speaking.

5. Stop often and have a conversation with Jesus. Ask him questions. Talk with him about what is going on in your life.

6. Thank Jesus for listening. Tell him you look forward to your next conversation with him.

FAITH VOCABULARY

Write a sentence that uses each of these terms correctly.

1. Bible
2. inspiration
3. canon of Sacred Scripture
4. oral tradition
5. literary genre
6. covenant

MAIN IDEAS

Choose either (a) or (b) from each set of items. Write a brief paragraph to answer each of your choices.

1. (a) Explain why we say the Bible is God's own word to us.

   (b) Describe the role of the human writers of the Bible.

2. (a) Describe the story of God's covenant with humankind.

   (b) Compare Sacred Scripture and Sacred Tradition. Include the concept *deposit of faith* in your response.

CRITICAL THINKING

Using what you have learned in this chapter, explain this statement:

"The Bible is no mere book, but a living creature, with a power that conquers all."

NAPOLEON BONAPARTE

FAMILY DISCUSSION

How is family life a covenant between family members?

For more ideas on ways your family can live your faith, visit the "Faith First for Families" page at **www.FaithFirst.com**. Click on the Teen Center and read this week's interactive story.

The Man Born Blind

A Scripture Story

FAITH FOCUS

How does the Gospel story of Jesus healing the man born blind help us live our faith in Jesus?

FAITH VOCABULARY

Fourth Gospel · miracle
Book of Signs

What are your favorite stories? What makes them your favorites?

A story is written for an audience. Some writers write for young people. When an author writes for a special audience, the writer will tell a story in a certain way, emphasizing different details that relate to the audience, or readers for whom the story has been written.

Each of the writers of the four Gospels, or the Evangelists, also wrote for a special audience. While each of the Gospels was written for a special audience, they all present the life, Passion, death, and Resurrection of Jesus, and the meaning of his life.

What is your favorite Gospel story? Why?

"I do believe, Lord."
JOHN 9:38

The Gospel According to John

The Gospel according to John was probably written between A.D. 90 and 100. John selected events from the life of Jesus that would have special meaning to his readers. John tells his readers:

> Now Jesus did many other signs in the presence of [his] disciples that are not written in this book. But these are written that you may [come to] believe that Jesus is the Messiah, the Son of God, and that through this belief you may have life in his name.
>
> JOHN 20:30–31

The **Fourth Gospel**, as John's account of the Gospel is also called, was first written for a community of Jewish Christians. They were being excluded from the worship life of the Jewish community because they had become believers in Jesus. The Fourth Gospel encourages and strengthens this early Christian community to have hope and to keep their faith and belief in Jesus Christ.

Reading John's Gospel helped many early Christians strengthen their faith in God and in Jesus. They came "to see," a phrase John uses to mean "to believe," that Jesus was the Messiah, the Son of God.

Describe the audience for whom the Fourth Gospel was first written.

Twelfth-century illuminated manuscript, Gospel according to John

The Book of Signs

John the Evangelist makes brilliant use of literary techniques. These techniques draw the audience deeply into the unfolding action of the story.

The first part of the Gospel according to John is also called the **Book of Signs.** This part of John's Gospel includes many stories of **miracles,** or signs, that Jesus performed. Each miracle story is intended to strengthen the faith of its readers and listeners in God.

The story of the man born blind in John's Gospel is an example of a miracle story. It is also an example of why Scripture scholars describe John as a skilled playwright. Read this story as a play.

Act 1: The Healing of the Man
(John 9:1–12)

Act 2: Dialogue and Interrogation
(John 9:13–41)

Act 3: A Soliloquy, or monologue, by Jesus
(John 10:1–18)

Notice how there are no more than two characters or groups of characters who speak on stage at the same time.

Describe a time when someone has used a story to help you understand something important.

Miracle of the multiplication of the loaves, John 6:1–15.

Miracle of changing water into wine at Cana, John 2:1–12.

FAITH CONNECTION

What groups of people in your community or what groups you have heard or read about in the news may have felt excluded because of what they believe?

_____

_____

_____

31

The Curing of the Man Born Blind, Artist unknown.

The Man Born Blind

The story of the man born blind begins with a recounting of this miracle of healing (see John 9:1–12).

Act 1:
The Healing of the Man

Jesus and his disciples had been driven from the Temple area. As they were walking, they came upon a man who had been born blind, sitting near the Pool of Siloam. This was a place in which many used to bathe themselves. Seeing the man the disciples asked Jesus:

> "Rabbi, who sinned, this man or his parents, that he was born blind?" Jesus answered, "Neither he nor his parents sinned; it is so that the works of God might be made visible through him. We have to do the works of the one who sent me while it is day. Night is coming when no one can work. While I am in the world, I am the light of the world." When he had said this, he spat on the ground and made clay with the saliva, and smeared the clay on his eyes, and said to him, "Go wash in the Pool of Siloam" (which means Sent). So he went and washed, and came back able to see. JOHN 9:2–7

Act 2:
Dialogue and Interrogation

The second act of the play (John 9:13–41) begins when others who knew the man asked how he could now see. After the man told them what Jesus had done, his neighbors and others brought the man to the Pharisees who also asked the man how it was that he could now see.

When the man told the Pharisees what Jesus had done, they did not believe him. They called the man's parents to testify that the man had truly been born blind. The man's parents refused to change their story. The Pharisees called the man back a second time and interrogated him. Refusing to budge, the man stood up to the Pharisees, saying:

> "If this man were not from God, he would not be able to do anything." They answered and said to him, "You were born totally in sin, and are you trying to teach us?" Then they threw him out.   JOHN 9:33–34

The action reached a climax as Jesus sought out the man and asked him about his faith and belief.

> When Jesus heard that they had thrown him out, he found him and said, "Do you believe in the Son of Man?" He answered and said, "Who is he, sir, that I may believe in him?" Jesus said to him, "You have seen him and the one speaking with you is he." He said, "I do believe, Lord," and he worshiped him.   JOHN 9:35–38

The man expressed his faith in Jesus by using the divine title, saying, "I do believe, Lord" (John 9:38), and he worshiped him.

In the interrogation of the man, the authorities tried to intimidate him. He remained steadfast. As a result, "they threw him out" (John 9:34). This is surely a deliberate allusion to the fate suffered by Jewish Christians for whom the Evangelist is writing.

Read Act 3, a soliloquy by Jesus, in John 10:1–18. Share with the class how this passage helps you understand the story of the man born blind.

Blind Man Washes in the Pool of Siloam. James J. Tissot (1836–1902), French artist.

Faith in Jesus

The early Christians believed there was more to this story than just a miracle of a man gaining his sight. The physical effects of a miracle—for example, the restoring of sight to the man born blind—cannot be explained by any natural causes. In the Gospel a miracle is a wonderful sign of God working among people, inviting us to believe and trust in him. Recall what the writer of the Fourth Gospel wrote:

Now Jesus did many other signs in the presence of [his] disciples that are not written in this book. But these are written that you may [come to] believe that Jesus is the Messiah, the Son of God, and that through this belief you may have life in his name.

JOHN 20:30–31

Faith in Jesus is the focus of this story. John's deepest concern was to help his readers explore the meaning of that faith. In the story of the man's journey from physical blindness to spiritual sight, the reader recognizes someone who receives physical sight, sees with the eyes of faith, and comes to new life in Christ. Those who come to the light and believe in Jesus will not perish but will enjoy eternal life.

What does the story of the man born blind teach us about faith?

Children of the Light

We can see ourselves as actors in John's drama about the man born blind and the unseeing Pharisees. The story helps us recognize that we face the same choices as the man born blind and the Pharisees did. God acts in our lives. We too are called to express our faith in Jesus.

The Holy Spirit invites us to choose the light over the dark and to profess our faith in God acting in our lives. The Holy Spirit invites us to faith even when professing and living that faith means facing opposition, even when it means being "excluded" from the "in" crowd.

FAITH CONNECTION

What could you do today to show others that your faith in Jesus is strong?

_____

_____

_____

_____

_____

OUR CHURCH
MAKES A DIFFERENCE

Christian Initiation

The Church has always used symbols and symbolic actions to invite us to faith. In the celebration of the "Rite of Acceptance into the Order of Catechumens," which is part of the *Rite of Christian Initiation of Adults*, the Catholic Church signs the forehead and senses of the candidate, or person wishing to become a member of the Catholic Church.

CELEBRANT: [Names], Christ has called you to be his friends. Always remember him and be faithful to him.

Therefore, I mark your forehead with the sign of the cross. It is the sign of Christians; let it remind you always of Christ and how much he loves you.

The senses of the candidates are now also signed one at at time either by the celebrant, parents, sponsors, or catechists as the celebrant prays for the candidate.

Each day we are called to live our faith in Jesus. Describe how you might use your eyes, ears, lips, hands, and heart to show you are a follower of Jesus Christ.

WHAT DIFFERENCE
Does Faith Make in My Life?

Obstacles to Seeing with Eyes of Faith

Not only did the man born blind receive his sight, but his eyes were opened to see things differently. Sometimes our eyes are clouded, and there are things that blind us and keep us from seeing clearly. Here are some common obstacles that can prevent you from seeing with eyes of faith. The first step to overcoming these obstacles is to be aware of them.

Close-Minded

Have you ever met a close-minded person, someone who believes that they are always right? Someone who thinks that they have all the answers all the time?

Open–minded means to be open to listen to other people's opinions, to think about and reflect on them, and evaluate those opinions. Try not to be blinded to new insights that could help you grow in understanding and to make better decisions.

Substance Abuse

Alcohol. It may seem cool to sneak a drink, but it is not. Alcohol is a drug that can be extremely dangerous, especially for young people. It can have harmful effects on your growth and development as well as your relationships and your decision-making skills. It can be very addictive.

Other drugs. The use of illegal drugs and the misuse of prescription and over-the-counter drugs can keep you from seeing reality. They prevent you from dealing honestly with whatever emotions you are feeling. You may believe that the abuse and misuse of drugs will not affect you, that they will not be able to hook you, but they can and they will. Drugs are so powerful that they can blind you from living a healthy life. They can blind you to God's presence in your life.

Self-Centered

You are blind to people and the world around you if you are totally absorbed with yourself, your clothes, your possessions. You are not meant to live only for yourself. While you need to take care of yourself and your things, you also need to reach out and be in healthy relationships with others.

"Came to See"

The blind man "came to see." The man began to see with the eyes of faith. He began to see all the wonderful things in his life and in his world. The gift of faith enables us to see and recognize God's presence in our life and in the lives of others. Through the gift of faith God invites us to open both our minds and hearts to him.

By overcoming these obstacles— by choosing to be open-minded rather than close-minded, by making choices for your better health, and by striving to be in good relationships with God, others, and all of creation—you will be able to see with eyes of faith. Keep your eyes open to the wonderful things that God wants to share with you.

Faith·Decision

Design a bulletin board titled "Eyes of Faith." Describe or sketch photos you would use to portray young people overcoming obstacles discussed on these pages.

- How would an open-minded person see a homeless person?
- When you hear about or see a friend using tobacco, alcohol, or illegal drugs, what is your response?
- When you see a friend disconnected from others, what do you see?

This week I will try to evaluate situations with the eyes of faith by

_____

_____

_____

PRAY and REVIEW

Signing of the Senses

Celebrant:

I (we) mark your ears with the sign of the cross: hear the words of Christ.

I (we) mark your eyes with the sign of the cross: see the works of Christ.

I (we) mark your lips with the sign of the cross: speak as Christ would speak.

I (we) mark the sign of the cross over your heart: make your heart the home of Christ.

I (we) mark your shoulders with the sign of the cross: be strong with the strength of Christ.

I (we) mark your hands with the sign of the cross: touch others with the gentleness of Christ.

I (we) mark your feet with the sign of the cross: walk in the way of Christ.

The sign of the cross is now traced above the whole person as the celebrant prays aloud:

Celebrant:

I (we) place you entirely under the sign of Christ's cross in the name of the Father, and of the Son, and of the Holy Spirit: live with Jesus now and for ever.

Candidates:

Amen.

BASED ON "SIGNING OF THE OTHER SENSES," RITE OF CHRISTIAN INITIATION OF ADULTS, 56

FAITH VOCABULARY

Use each of these terms correctly in a sentence.

1. Fourth Gospel
2. Book of Signs
3. miracle

MAIN IDEAS

Choose either (a) or (b) from each set of items. Write a brief paragraph to answer each of your choices.

1. (a) Describe the main focus of the four Gospels.
   (b) Why was the Gospel according to John written?

2. (a) Why is the first part of the Gospel according to John called the Book of Signs?
   (b) Compare the story of Jesus' curing the man born blind with the gift of faith.

CRITICAL THINKING

Using what you have learned in this chapter, briefly explain this statement:
When we look at the world and ourselves with the eyes of faith, we see things in a unique way.

FAMILY DISCUSSION

How can seeing with eyes of faith guide our family in the way we respond to one another?

For more ideas on ways your family can live your faith, visit the "Faith First for Families" page at **www.FaithFirst.com**. Read the Bible story on the Teen Center this week.

The Mystery of Creation

4

Why does reflecting in faith on the diversity within creation help us come to know more and more about who God is?

FAITH VOCABULARY

attribute

divine Providence

eternal

soul

omnipresence

Who do you know who is an image of one of their parents?

Think about children who closely resemble one or the other of their parents. There is no doubt they are all members of the same family.

We can apply the same connections to God and creation. Taking a close look at creation, we can get a glimpse of God, who is the source of *all* creation.

What might a mountain or sunset or field of wheat tell you about God?

God looked at everything he had made, and he found it very good.
Genesis 1:31

God the Creator

God the Almighty One

When we open our eyes and minds to ponder the majesty and the mystery of creation, we cannot help but be led to a sense of awe before the Creator whose image is traced in such vastness and diversity.

Paul the Apostle writes:

> Ever since the creation of the world, his invisible attributes of eternal power and divinity have been able to be understood and perceived in what he has made. ROMANS 1:20

We use the word **attribute** to classify some of the things we have come to know about God. An attribute is a quality or characteristic that belongs to a person or thing. The many attributes the Church uses for God only give us a glimpse into the infinite mystery of God who has freely chosen to reveal himself to us.

God Is the Creator

In the Nicene Creed we profess:
I believe in one God
the Father almighty,
maker of heaven and earth,
of all things visible and invisible.

God is our Creator and the Creator of all things. God freely, directly, and without any help created "heaven and earth" (Apostles' Creed), "all things visible and invisible" (Nicene Creed) out of nothing.

Before God created the world, only God existed—no one else, nothing else. There were no angels, no humans. No eagles soared over mountaintops, nor did dolphins playfully splash in the oceans alongside whales. There were no sheep grazing on hillside pastures, nor otters building dams to divert a flowing stream. Majestic redwoods did not reach up to the sky, and wheat fields did not blow in the wind.

There was nothing and no one until God, out of love, freely chose to create. Now creatures share in his goodness and beauty and tell of the glory that belongs to God alone.

Describe what the Church means when we profess our faith in God, the Creator of heaven and earth.

God Is One

At the heart of God's revelation of himself is that he is One. In the Old Testament we read:

> "Hear, O Israel! The LORD is our God, the LORD alone! Therefore, you shall love the LORD, your God, with all your heart, and with all your soul, and with all your strength."
>
> DEUTERONOMY 6:4–5

The Israelites came to know God to be One. They believed, unlike their neighbors, that there is only one true God who is the Creator of everything.

The belief in one God is called monotheism. It was far different from what the neighbors of the Israelites and the majority of the people who lived in Old Testament times believed about God. Most believed there were many gods. We call this belief polytheism.

God Is Eternal

The Israelites also came to know that God alone has no beginning and no end. We use the attribute **eternal,** or everlasting, to describe this characteristic of God. God alone always was and always will be. The attribute belongs to God alone.

What does it mean that God is one and eternal?

Did you Know...

Saint Teresa of Avila (1515–1582) was a Spanish mystic who is one of the few saints the Church has honored with the title "Doctor of the Church." Teresa's life may be summarized as a prayerful journey in search of communion with God, the only true source of happiness. This journey is brilliantly described in her autobiographical masterpiece, *The Interior Castle*. Saint Teresa of Avila is the patron saint of Spain. The Church celebrates her feast day on October 15.

FAITH CONNECTION

Make a symbol for the first part of the Nicene Creed. Use the symbol to teach the creed to a younger group of children.

God is love, and whoever remains in love remains in God and God in him.

1 John 4:16

God Is Truth

In reflecting on creation and God's word to his people, the inspired writers of the Bible share with us their belief that God alone is the source of all truth and knowledge.

> "And now, LORD God, you are God and your words are truth." 2 SAMUEL 7:28

Because God is the source of all creation, all truth ultimately comes from him. God is Truth itself.

We believe and trust everything the living God reveals to us. He gives us his word, and his word is always true. God always keeps his word. Under the guidance of the Holy Spirit, the Church guides us in understanding the meaning of the truth that God reveals.

God Is Always Present

God's people in the Old Testament also use the term *presence* to describe God. This expresses their belief that God does not create and abandon his people. He is always present to all of his creation. Without God's presence, creation would cease to exist.

We call this attribute of God his **omnipresence.** We believe the almighty power and loving care of God, or **divine Providence**, is always with us.

> Though the mountains leave their place
> and the hills be shaken,
> my love shall never leave you.
> ISAIAH 54:10

God Is Love

By sending the Son, who would freely choose to die for us, God revealed the innermost mystery, or secret, about himself:

> God is love. 1 JOHN 4:8

God created us and saved us. He chose us to be his people because of who he is: love.

What does it mean that God is Truth and always present with us?

Created in God's Image

The first story of creation in the Book of Genesis (see Genesis 1:1–2:4a) makes it clear that people are the summit of God's creation. After God finished creating the universe and saw how good it was, he said,

"Let us make man in our image, after our likeness." GENESIS 1:26

The writer of the second story of creation in Genesis (see Genesis 2:4b–25) describes the creation of the first human this way:

[T]he LORD God formed man out of the clay of the ground and blew into his nostrils the breath of life, and so man became a living being. GENESIS 2:7

Made from the clay of the earth, we have received the breath of life from God.

God created us with a body and a **soul**. Our soul is the spiritual part of who we are that is immortal, or never dies. God has given us an intelligence and a free will. These powers are gifts from God that give us the power to know and love God, other people, and ourselves. This unique privilege is ours alone among all the creatures of earth. From the first moment of our existence these wonderful gifts show that God created us to know and love him now and forever in heaven.

Male and Female

When we read or listen to the first creation story, God also tells us that he did not create us to be alone. There is another side to us. We have been created to live in community. We read:

God created man in his image;
in the divine image he
created him;
male and female he created
them. GENESIS 1:27

Men and women share equally the honor and dignity of being made in God's image and likeness. Men and women have been created to live as partners. It is part of the divine plan that a man and a woman join together in marriage. This partnership of a man and a woman, the family, is the first and basic form of community. Created in the image and likeness of God, a married couple is a sign of God's life-giving love for us.

Describe the relationship between men and women in God's plan of creation.

Original Justice

God created the first humans in the state of original justice. The word *justice* means "being in the right order." God created us in a life-giving relationship with him, with one another, and with all creation.

The Book of Genesis (see Genesis 3:1–24) tells us that the first humans, Adam and Eve, lost that state of original justice not only for themselves but for all human beings. They committed the original, or first, sin. They knowingly and freely rejected God's plan of creation. They knew God's plan and chose to replace it with their own. We call this story in Genesis the Fall.

New Creation

We know the consequence of that choice of Adam and Eve. The rest of the Bible is the story of God's commitment to restore his original plan. It is the story of God's plan of salvation, the deliverance of humanity and all creation from the power of sin and death. The plan of God's loving goodness will be fulfilled in the new creation in Jesus Christ, the Son of God made man. He is the new Adam. (See 1 Corinthians 15:20–28.)

We exist to share in the beauty and goodness and love of God. This is the glory for which God has created us. This plan and promise will be fulfilled in the new creation in Christ when Christ comes again in glory at the end of time.

FAITH CONNECTION

Work with a group. Write the name of your class in the center of a circle. Around the circle, list all the ways that your class tries to cooperate with God's plan for creation.

OUR CHURCH
MAKES A DIFFERENCE

Recreating All Things in Christ

The students, faculty, and families of Bishop Lynch High School in Dallas, Texas, work diligently to put into practice the faith they talk about and study in school. One way they do this is by building life-giving relationships within their school community and within the larger civic and Church community of which their school is a part. These life-giving relationships are strengthened through a peer ministry program called "Peer Helpers" and through participation in the "Hearts & Hammers" project.

Peer Ministry

At the beginning of the school year, Peer Helpers serve as ambassadors. They welcome new students, answer questions, guide the lost, and make everyone feel comfortable. Peer Helpers also sponsor a one-day camp for new students to help them become familiar with their school, one another, and the entire school community. Other peer ministry programs include a one-on-one tutoring program and the Student Symposium, where students can openly discuss school issues, seek advice, and discover solutions to problems they identify.

Hearts & Hammers

Members of the Bishop Lynch community are also involved in the civic community. They clean area parks, paint over graffiti, work with area food banks, and join with the Hearts & Hammers project. They join with other volunteers to renovate the homes of the elderly, the disabled, those families living immediately above or below the poverty level, and homeowners who are in danger of losing their homes because they are physically or financially unable to keep the property in compliance with code requirements.

In what new ways could your class be a living image of God the Creator for others?

WHAT DIFFERENCE
Does Faith Make in My Life?

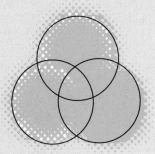

Building Relationships

You have been created in the image and likeness of God, who is one God in three Persons. *Relationship* is a word we think about when we reflect on the meaning of the Holy Trinity for our own lives.

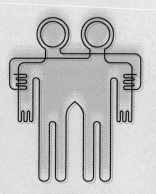

You have been created to live in relationship with God and with others. Jesus summed up this truth this way: We are to love God with our whole mind, heart, soul, and strength. We are to love our neighbor as ourselves. (See Matthew 22:34–40.)

You now live in many relationships. What are some of those relationships?

_____

_____

_____

Healthy Relationships

As you grow you continually need to develop skills that help you live in healthy relationships with others. Respect and life-giving are two of the most important qualities of healthy relationships.

- Respect honors the dignity of yourself and others. Developing respect in our relationships works toward eliminating prejudice, violence, and all other forms of verbal, physical, and spiritual harm from our relationships.

- People in life-giving relationships support one another. We develop one another's gifts and talents.

Describe some of the ways that respect is part of your relationship with others.

_____

_____

_____

_____

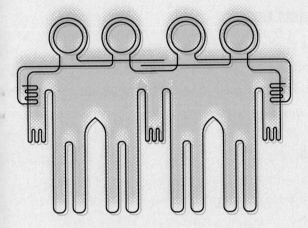

Signs of a Healthy Relationship

Respect for
Each other
Loving, loyal, listening
Attentiveness, attitude of caring
Trust of each other
Interest in each other's
    well-being
Openness to each other, freely
    sharing and expressing opinions
Nurturing and supporting each
    other to be one's best
Sharing hopes, dreams, fears,
    beliefs, spirituality
Humor
Integrity, honor and loyalty, treating
    others as you wish to be treated
Positive attitude, play fair, disagree
    peacefully
Skills that you need to practice.

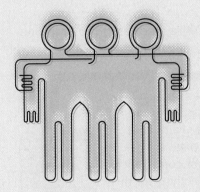

Faith· Decision

- Choose one of the signs of a healthy relationship. Select magazine photos that illustrate the sign you have chosen. Combine your photos with those of the other students to create a "Healthy Relationship" collage.

- Think of one thing you can do this week to work at building a healthy relationship with someone. I will

_____

_____

_____

PRAY and REVIEW

Praise God

Leader:

Lord, holy Father,
   almighty and eternal God,
we praise you as the God
   of creation,
as the Father of Jesus,
   the Savior of the world,
in whose image we seek to live.

All:

Holy, Holy, Holy!
Jesus loved the children
   of the lands he walked
and enriched them with
   his witness of justice and truth.

Leader:

Jesus lived and died
   that we might be reborn
      in the Spirit
and filled with love for all people.

All:

Holy, Holy, Holy Lord
   God of hosts.
Heaven and earth are full
   of your glory.
   Hosanna in the highest.
Blessed is he who comes in
   the name of the Lord.
Hosanna in the highest.

BASED ON THE PREFACE FOR INDEPENDENCE DAY
ROMAN MISSAL

FAITH VOCABULARY

Define each of these faith terms:

1. attributes
2. eternal
3. omnipresence
4. divine Providence
5. soul

MAIN IDEAS

Choose either (a) or (b) from each set of items. Write a brief paragraph to answer each of your choices.

1. (a) Explain what the Church means when it teaches that God is the Creator of all, seen and unseen.
   (b) Name and explain two attributes of God.

2. (a) Explain what it means to say that people are created in the image and likeness of God.
   (b) Compare the terms *original justice* and *salvation*.

CRITICAL THINKING

Using what you have learned in this chapter, briefly explain this statement:

[Christ] is the image of the invisible God,
   the firstborn of all creation.
For in him were created all things in heaven
   and on earth.   COLOSSIANS 1:15–16

FAMILY DISCUSSION

What are some things we can do to help one another grow in our knowledge and love of God?

For more ideas on ways your family can live your faith, visit the "Faith First for Families" page at **www.FaithFirst.com**. Check out the extra activity for this chapter on the Teen Center.

God: Father, Son, and Holy Spirit

FAITH FOCUS

How have Christians come to explain the mystery of the Holy Trinity?

FAITH VOCABULARY

Holy Trinity

dogma of faith

What recent scientific discoveries intrigue you?

Scientists struggle to come up with solutions to the mysteries that fill the universe. As they gather more data and weigh the evidence, researchers make breakthroughs in their knowledge and understanding of these mysteries.

The deepest mystery of all is the mystery of God. God has revealed himself to us so we can come to know who he truly is.

From your prayer, your study of the Scriptures, and the teachings of the Church, what have you come to know about God?

The Holy Trinity, mosaic

"The Advocate, the holy Spirit that the Father will send in my name —he will teach you everything."
JOHN 14:26

49

The Mystery of the Holy Trinity

The Mystery of God

The word *mystery* has a special meaning when we speak of God as mystery. It means more than the solvable problems posed and solved by scientists. When we speak of God as mystery, we mean that we can never fully comprehend or fully grasp God. Only because he reveals himself can we come to know a glimpse of the truth of God's inner life and his plan for our salvation.

God the Holy Trinity

The central truth that God has revealed about himself is that he is one God in three divine Persons. We call this truth about God the mystery of the **Holy Trinity.**

Our Christian belief in the Holy Trinity is based on God's revelation of himself. From Sacred Scripture and Sacred Tradition we come to know and believe that God, who created and saves us and shares his life and love with us, is one God who is Father, Son, and Holy Spirit.

The Holy Trinity, stained-glass window

"I will ask the Father, and he will give you ... the Spirit of truth."

John 14:16–17

Did you Know...

At the First Council of Nicaea (A.D. 325), Athanasius (d. 373), the bishop of Alexandria, was one of the strongest defenders of the Church's teachings on the Holy Trinity. Angered by Athanasius's unwavering stand against the erroneous teachings of Arius (c. 250–336), Emperor Constantine, a friend of Arius, took the side of Athanasius's enemies and sent him into exile. Athanasius is called the Father of Orthodoxy, a word meaning "true teaching." Athanasius is honored as a saint and a Doctor of the Church. The Church celebrates his feast day on May 2.

Jesus and God the Father

The writers of the Gospels identify God as the Father of Jesus Christ 170 times—42 times in Matthew, 4 times in Mark, 15 times in Luke, and 109 times in John. In the face of his disciples' struggle to understand who he was, Jesus asked:

"Do you not believe that I am in the Father and the Father is in me?" JOHN 14:10

The Apostles and other disciples came to understand that Jesus was putting himself on a par with God the Father. Jesus is the Son of God who is equally God as the Father is God.

Jesus and the Holy Spirit

In his final words to his disciples at the Last Supper, Jesus taught his disciples about the Holy Spirit. He said:

"And I will ask the Father, and he will give you another Advocate to be with you always, the Spirit of truth." JOHN 14:16–17

The first Christians gradually came to confess their belief in one God who is mysteriously Father, Son, and Holy Spirit. This profession of faith became the norm, or standard, by which someone became a follower of Jesus Christ.

FAITH CONNECTION

Write a short prayer to God the Father or to God the Son or to God the Holy Spirit. In your prayer share something you have come to believe about that divine Person of the Holy Trinity.

_____

_____

_____

_____

One God in Three Persons

Beginning in the fourth century the bishops of the Church began meeting in a series of councils at Nicaea (325), Constantinople (381), Ephesus (431), and Chalcedon (451). One of the main purposes of these councils was to discuss and explain the authentic beliefs of the Church about Jesus Christ and his relationship to the Father and the Holy Spirit.

At the center of this debate was Arius, who asked, "How can Jesus be God and the Father also be God?" Because he could not solve his dilemma, Arius taught that Jesus was not truly God. He taught that Jesus was created by God the Father superior in dignity to any other creature, but that Jesus was not equal to God the Father.

Nature and Person

At these councils the Church explained the Christian belief and teaching on the **Holy Trinity.** They taught:

1. There is only one divine *nature* equally and totally shared by the Father, Son, and Holy Spirit. There is only one God.

2. The Father is not the Son or the Holy Spirit; the Son is not the Father or the Holy Spirit; and the Holy Spirit is not the Father or the Son.

3. The relationship of the divine Persons—Father, Son, and Holy Spirit—is so close, it unites them as one God.

The mystery of the Holy Trinity is a **dogma of faith.** A dogma is a truth taught by the Church as revealed by God. While this great mystery of our faith, the Holy Trinity, is difficult to explain in words, we believe this truth about God because he has revealed this truth about himself to us.

The Work of the Holy Trinity

Our language seems to limit specific works of God to a particular Person of the Holy Trinity. For example, in the Nicene Creed we credit, or attribute, the work of creation to God the Father. We profess:

I believe in one God
the Father almighty,
maker of heaven and earth,
of all things visible and invisible.

NICENE CREED

We talk about God's work among us as if each divine Person has a particular work. The truth is that just as God is one, God's work is also one. God's whole plan of loving-kindness is the work of the one God—Father, Son, and Holy Spirit. The Father is never separated from the Son and the Holy Spirit; the Son is never separated from the Father and the Holy Spirit; the Holy Spirit is never separated from the Father and the Son.

How would you summarize the kinds of work that the Holy Trinity does?

We call the works of God the **divine missions** of the three Persons of the Holy Trinity. We attribute the work of creation to the Father, who sent us his Son; the work of salvation to the Son, who came and lived among us and was raised from the dead; the work of sanctification, or our holiness, to the Holy Spirit, who is the love of God sent to us by the Father and the Son.

The Work of Creation

Let us now take a look at the work of creation as the work of the Trinity.

God the Father

While we attribute the work of creation to God the Father, creation is truly the work of the Trinity. A closer reading of Scripture helps us see that the Son and the Holy Spirit are just as much involved in creation as the Father.

God the Son

The Gospel according to John opens:

In the beginning was
the Word, . . .
and the Word was God. . . .

JOHN 1:1

The Word of God is the Son of God. Echoing the Genesis story, Saint John the Evangelist passes on the Church's belief that the work of the Father is also the work of the Son. He writes,

All things came to be
through him,
and without him nothing
came to be.   JOHN 1:3

God the Holy Spirit

In the Genesis account of creation, we read:

[T]he earth was a formless wasteland, and darkness covered the abyss, while a mighty wind swept over the waters.   GENESIS 1:2

We use the English word *wind* to translate the Hebrew word *ruah*. Christians have come to see this image as indicating the work of the Holy Spirit in creation.

The work of God among us is always the work of the Holy Trinity. There is one God who creates us and saves us and sanctifies us. There is one God who invites us to share in the life of the Holy Trinity here on earth and after death in the eternal life of heaven. This is God's loving plan of creation, salvation, and sanctification.

The Work of Creation,
contemporary stained-glass

FAITH CONNECTION

List ways that you and others cooperate with God's work in the world. Tell your class one thing you have done and one thing you have seen done by others to prepare for the coming of God's kingdom.

_____

_____

_____

_____

OUR CHURCH
MAKES A DIFFERENCE

The Christian Family

The Christian family is a community of persons created by God in the image of God. It is a community of faith, hope, and love that is a sign of God's work and love among us.

A Community of Faith

In our family we first learn about God and grow in our trust in his love for us. As we grow, our family teaches us many ways to live our faith. In our families we witness the faith of our parents, grandparents, and other family members who live the faith in their normal everyday lives.

A Community of Love

The family is where we come to know and experience what love is. Through the sacrifices our parents make for us we come to know there is no limit to God's love for us. The hugs, the smiles, the kind words lead us to see that God is love.

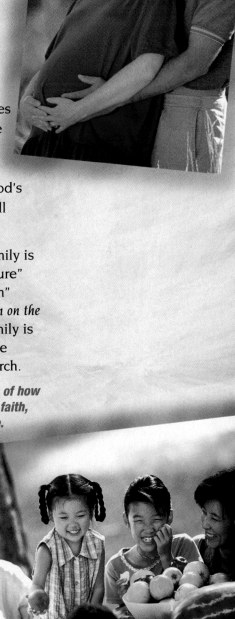

A Community of Hope

It is with our family that we discover our talents and gifts and take up our responsibilities to build a community of justice and peace, compassion and forgiveness. We become people of hope, trusting in God's promises that his kingdom will triumph.

The Christian family is a "church in miniature" or "domestic church" (*Dogmatic Constitution on the Church*, 11). The family is a living image of the mystery of the Church.

Give examples of how families show faith, hope, and love.

WHAT DIFFERENCE
Does Faith Make in My Life?

Balancing Relationships

In this chapter you learned that there is one God who is Father, Son, and Holy Spirit. Your relationship with God gives direction to your relationships with family, friends, neighbors, and others.

Balancing your relationships with friends, family, and others is not always easy. But it can be done.

As teenagers you are seeking more independence. This may at times seem to cause conflict in your relationship with your parents. Learning how to handle the increased personal responsibility that comes with increased independence may sometimes seem exciting. At other times it may be downright scary. Balancing your relationships within your family is a normal part of growing up. What is not part of the normal process is deliberately upsetting or destroying the harmony within your family life.

Skills to Help Maintain Balance in the Family

How can you balance getting your needs met as a growing teenager with meeting your responsibilities as a member of your family? Learning family-living skills will help.

- **MUTUAL RESPECT** is honoring each family member's gifts and talents. It is the give and take, the back and forth, and the blending of the ME and WE that makes a healthy family work.

- **COMMUNICATION** is another way to keep balance in your family. The members of your family each have their own views about things. A very good way to express your opinion is to use "I feel" statements. For example, "I feel angry when Johnny monopolizes the TV. I feel we should take a vote on what program we can all watch." By using "I feel" statements you can express your feelings and views calmly without forcing them on other family members. This approach can lead to respectful family discussions.

- **MEETING INDIVIDUAL RESPONSIBILITIES** contributes to family life. Your family is not simply a place where you stop by to eat and sleep and refuel. The other members of your family depend on you as much as you depend on them. Taking ownership and fulfilling your responsibilities within your family go hand in hand with handling your growing need and desire for independence.

- **COOPERATION** happens when family members look out for one another. Family is a "together" thing.

There are no perfect families and no perfect family members, but you and every member of your family are very special and very important to your family. Remember that God loves each and every member of your family. God is with your family, giving you help and support in your efforts to love one another.

Faith Decision

- Choose a partner. Role-play a parent and a teenage family member. Discuss one of the following topics: music, curfew, allowance, or a topic of your choosing.

- Practice using "I feel" statements as you and your partner role-play the topic you selected. Then reverse the roles.

This week I will try to balance my need for independence with my family responsibilities by

_____

_____

_____

_____

_____

_____.

Apostles' Creed

Group 1:
I believe in God,
the Father almighty,
Creator of heaven and earth,
and in Jesus Christ, his only Son,
our Lord,

Group 2:
who was conceived
by the Holy Spirit,
born of the Virgin Mary,
suffered under Pontius Pilate,
was crucified, died and
was buried;
he descended into hell;
on the third day he rose again
from the dead;
he ascended into heaven,
and is seated at the
right hand of God
the Father almighty;
from there he will come to
judge the living and the dead.

Group 3:
I believe in the Holy Spirit,
the holy catholic Church,
the communion of saints,
the forgiveness of sins,
the resurrection of the body,
and life everlasting. Amen.

FAITH VOCABULARY

Define each of these faith terms:

1. Holy Trinity   2. dogma of faith

MAIN IDEAS

Choose either (a) or (b) from each set of items. Write a brief paragraph to answer each of your choices.

1. (a) Describe the Church's teaching about the mystery of the Holy Trinity.
   (b) What do we learn about the Holy Trinity from the New Testament?

2. (a) Compare what Arius taught about the Trinity with the teachings of the early Church councils of Nicaea I, Constantinople, Ephesus, and Chalcedon.
   (b) Describe the work of creation, salvation, and sanctification as a work of the Trinity.

CRITICAL THINKING

Using what you have learned in this chapter, briefly explain this teaching of the Athanasian Creed:
We worship one God in the Trinity and the Trinity in unity.

FAMILY DISCUSSION

How do we as a family continue the work of God's creation in the world?

For more ideas on ways your family can live your faith, visit the "Faith First for Families" page at **www.FaithFirst.com**. The chapter review in the Teen Center will help you see what you have learned this week.

UNIT ONE
REVIEWREVIEW

A. The Best Response

Read each statement and circle the best answer.

1. What does the Church call God making himself known to us?
   A. divine Mystery
   B. divine Revelation
   C. divine Power
   D. divine Providence

2. What do we call the free, conscious human response to God's invitation to know and believe in him?
   A. hope
   B. love
   C. faith
   D. revelation

3. Which one of the following is not true about Jesus Christ?
   A. New Covenant
   B. Son of God
   C. Savior of the world
   D. Apostle

4. What do we call the belief in God's loving care and almighty power that is always with us?
   A. divine Providence
   B. divine Power
   C. divine Compassion
   D. divine Concern

5. What dogma of faith is stated in the statement, "There is one God in three divine Persons"?
   A. Holy Trinity
   B. Creation
   C. Incarnation
   D. Revelation

B. Matching Words and Phrases

Match the faith terms in column A with the descriptions in column B.

Column A

_____ 1. Book of Signs

_____ 2. literary genre

_____ 3. Fourth Gospel

_____ 4. covenant

_____ 5. Evangelists

_____ 6. Canon of Sacred Scripture

_____ 7. oral tradition

_____ 8. eternal

_____ 9. Sacred Scripture

_____ 10. deposit of faith

Column B

a. Gospel of John

b. list of books the Catholic Church teaches to be the inspired word of God

c. collection of writings inspired by God

d. God's revelation first passed on by word of mouth

e. different styles of writing

f. solemn agreement

g. first part of the Gospel of John

h. Sacred Scripture and Sacred Tradition

i. writers of the Gospels

j. everlasting, without beginning and without end

C. What I Have Learned

Using what you learned in Unit One, write a brief reflection about each of the following statements.

God is Truth.

God is the author of the Bible.

D. A Scripture Story

On a separate sheet of paper do the following.

Recall the Gospel story of the man born blind. In a group or on your own, develop a modern-day version of this story.

UNIT TWO
The Gift of Salvation

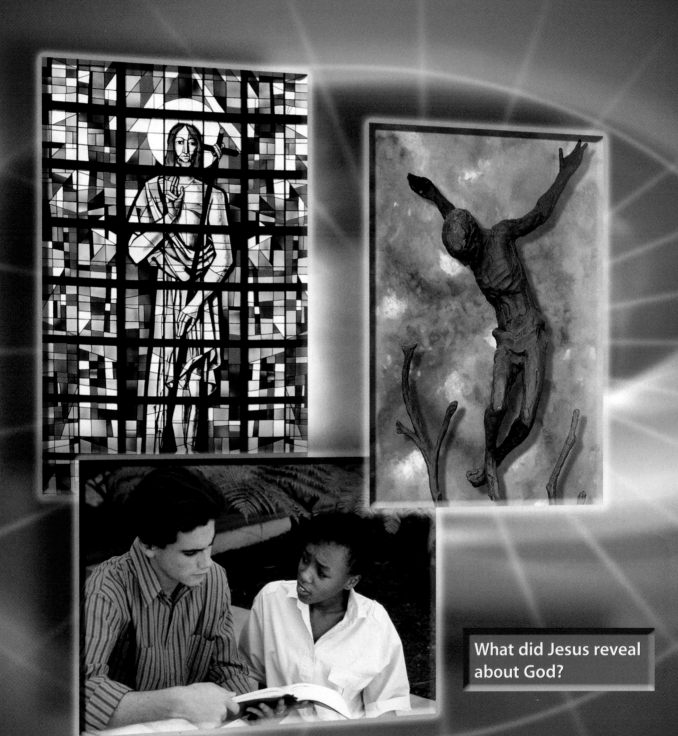

What did Jesus reveal about God?

Getting Ready

The Paschal Mystery

What do you know about the events of the Paschal Mystery of Christ?

Passion and death

_____

_____

Resurrection

_____

_____

Ascension

_____

_____

Questions I Have

What questions about Jesus' work of salvation do you hope these chapters will answer?

_____

_____

_____

_____

A Scripture Story

The Transfiguration

What do you know about this event from the life of Jesus?

Faith Vocabulary

Put an X next to the faith vocabulary terms that you know. Put a ? next to the faith vocabulary terms that you need to know more about.

____ Immaculate Conception

____ kingdom of God

____ Incarnation

____ Transfiguration

____ Messiah

____ original sin

____ Redemption

____ prophet

____ Resurrection

____ Ascension

____ Advocate

____ charism

Jesus Christ, the Son of God

FAITH FOCUS

How does the word *Incarnation* help us express our beliefs about Jesus Christ?

FAITH VOCABULARY

Immaculate Conception   YHWH

Lord   Incarnation

What might family members do or talk about as they wait for the birth of a new baby?

Excitement fills a family as they await the birth of a child. Family members carefully prepare for the newest member of the family to be born. A name is chosen. The crib is carefully made up.

God worked for centuries among his people, the Israelites, preparing the world for the birth of Jesus, the Son of God.

What does the Old Testament say that points to Jesus?

Madonna and Child, wood carving

But when the fullness of time had come, God sent his Son, born of a woman, born under the law.

GALATIANS 4:4

The Word Became Flesh

Preparing the Way

In ways that we still do not fully recognize, the Holy Spirit was always at work in human history, bringing about God's plan for the birth of the Savior, Jesus Christ. Paul the Apostle wrote:

> But when the fullness of time had come, God sent his Son, born of a woman, born under the law.
>
> GALATIANS 4:4

In the fullness of time, the Holy Spirit brought that plan about in Mary. By the action of the Holy Spirit in the Virgin Mary, she carried in her womb and gave birth to her only Son, Jesus (see Isaiah 7:14 and Matthew 1:22–23). The name *Jesus* means "God saves."

Blessed Mary, Ever-Virgin

We honor Mary as Blessed Mary, Ever-Virgin. Mary remained a virgin in conceiving her Son and in giving birth to him. After giving birth to Jesus, Mary remained a virgin her whole and entire life (see *Catechism of the Catholic Church*, 510).

The Virgin Mary is God's "favored one" (Luke 1:28), who was full of grace from the very beginning of her existence. Prepared by the grace of the Holy Spirit for the unique role that she would play in the divine plan, Mary is "the most excellent fruit of redemption." Because of the saving work of her Son, Mary was totally preserved from the stain of original sin. Neither did Mary commit any personal sin throughout her entire life. We call this the **Immaculate Conception** of Mary.

The Mother of God

Mary is truly the Mother of God because she is the mother of Jesus, the eternal Son of God. Through the work of the Holy Spirit, the Father gives the world his Son, whom the prophet Isaiah named *Immanuel* (see Isaiah 7:14), a Hebrew name that means "God with us." Through Mary and in her Son, Jesus, everything in the Old Testament converges and comes to fulfillment.

Describe the unique role of Mary in God's plan to send us the Savior.

The Annunciation, stained-glass

Jesus Is Truly God

All four Gospels make it clear that Jesus' relationship with God the Father is unique. The Gospel according to John, which begins with this profession of faith in Jesus, helps us understand that relationship.

> In the beginning was the Word,
>   and the Word was with God,
>   and the Word was God. . . .
> And the Word became flesh
>   and made his dwelling
>   among us.   JOHN 1:1, 14

Jesus is the eternally existing Word, who has always existed with the Father and the Holy Spirit. This has always been the faith of the Church. Jesus is true God and true man. He is truly and fully God. The Son of God took on flesh and became like us in all things except sin without giving up his divinity.

In the New Testament we read "Jesus Christ is Lord" (Philippians 2:11). This statement is a clear profession of the faith of the Church that Jesus is truly divine, or God.

The English word **Lord** translates the Greek word *kyrios*. *Kyrios* is also the Greek word the writers of the New Testament used to translate **YHWH**. YHWH are the Hebrew letters for the name God revealed for himself to Moses (see Exodus 3:14). It is the name that the writers of the Scriptures used only for God.

In order to be a Christian, a person must believe that Jesus Christ is truly the Son of God. The willingness and readiness of Christians to make this profession of faith in Jesus Christ is what makes us Christians.

FAITH ⋮ CONNECTION

Design a poster that proclaims the faith of the Church in Jesus.

Nativity detail. Bronze
doors, Church of the
Annunciation, Nazareth

Two Natures in One Person

Jesus is true God and true man. For
many centuries Christians searched
for the words to express this great
mystery of our faith. They knew that
Jesus was human—he lived and
walked among us; he died and was
raised from the dead and appeared
to his disciples before he ascended
to his Father. The evidence for this
is unmistakable. It is found not only
in the four accounts of the Gospel
but also in other Christian and
non-Christian writings.

But how can we express the faith
of the Church that Jesus is both
human and divine? What words can
possibly help others understand
this great mystery of faith?

Drawing from the language of the
philosophy of their day, the bishops
at the first two **ecumenical councils**
of the Church, Nicaea I (A.D. 325)
and Constantinople (A.D. 381), chose
the words *nature* and *person*. Our
nature makes us what we are.
Our person makes us who we are.
For example, our human nature is
what makes us human or gives us
our humanness. This is different
from the nature of an animal, like
a squirrel, which gives the squirrel
its "squirrelness."

In Jesus, the Incarnate Son of
God, there are two natures, a
human nature and a divine nature,
that are united in a single divine
Person, the Son of God, the
second Person of the Holy Trinity.
God the Son became truly and
fully human, or "took on flesh,"
without ceasing to be God. Out of
love, the Son of God became one
of us so that we might share in the
very life of God. We call this the
mystery of the **Incarnation**.

In Jesus there is the wonderful
union of the divine and human
natures in the one Person of God,
the Son who became one of us.
Jesus is true God and true man.
This teaching does not mean that
Jesus is part God and part man.
Jesus Christ is true God and true
man. The Son of God truly became
human while remaining truly God.

Jesus' entire life—his words and
actions, his gestures and silences,
everything about him—reveals the
mystery of God, who is Father and
Son and Holy Spirit, at work among
us. As one Christian put it: Jesus is,
in a real sense, the human face of
God among us.

*Describe how the Catholic Church
explains that Jesus is true God and
true man.*

The Infancy and Childhood of Jesus

Only the Gospel accounts of Matthew and Luke share with us stories about the infancy and childhood of Jesus. Each of these Infancy Narratives, as they are sometimes called, points to what the early Church came to believe about Jesus.

- Jesus' birth in Bethlehem points to him as the Savior whom God promised would come from the house of David (see Matthew 1:18–25, Luke 2:1–20).

- The adoration of Jesus by the Magi tells us that Jesus is the Savior of all people (see Matthew 2:1–12).
- The circumcision and naming of Jesus, the Savior, fulfill the Law of Moses and the Covenant that God entered into with the Israelites (see Luke 2:21).
- The flight of the Holy Family to Egypt and their return to Nazareth remind us of the Exodus. In Jesus all people would be freed from the power of sin (see Matthew 2:13–15, 19–23).
- The presentation of Jesus in the Temple in Jerusalem shows that he is dedicated to God and to the service of God (see Luke 2:22–40).
  - The finding of the boy Jesus in the Temple in Jerusalem teaches that doing his Father's will was the focus of Jesus' whole life on earth (see Luke 2:41–51).

What do the Infancy Narratives in the Gospel accounts of Matthew and Luke teach about Jesus?

The Public Life of Jesus

Details of the public life, or public ministry, of Jesus vary in each of the four accounts of the Gospel. Jesus' public ministry began with his baptism in the Jordan River by John the Baptist (see Luke 3:21–22).

Filled with the Holy Spirit, Jesus journeyed into the desert. There the tempter, the devil, tempted Jesus to betray his Father and the work given to him (see Matthew 4:1–11).

After rejecting the devil's offers, Jesus returned to Galilee and his hometown of Nazareth. There on the Sabbath he met in the synagogue with his neighbors as he had so often done. All eyes were riveted to Jesus. He stood and took the scroll of the prophet Isaiah.

He deliberately unrolled it, obviously looking for a particular passage, and finding the passage, he read aloud:

"The Spirit of the Lord is upon me,
because he has anointed me
to bring glad tidings to
the poor.
He has sent me to proclaim
liberty to captives
and recovery of sight to the
blind,
to let the oppressed go free,
and to proclaim a year acceptable
to the Lord." LUKE 4:18–19

Jesus' entire public ministry is marked by a tireless proclamation that the kingdom promised by God through the prophets "is at hand" (Mark 1:15).

FAITH CONNECTION

Discuss with a partner how Luke 4:18–19 calls Christians to live their Baptism. Summarize your discussion in this space.

_____

_____

_____

_____

_____

OUR CHURCH
MAKES A DIFFERENCE

Symbols for Jesus Christ

From the beginning of the Church Christians have created and used symbols that help us understand and express the Church's faith in Jesus Christ. Christian symbols express in images the same Gospel truths about Jesus that the Bible and the Church also express in words.

Chi-Rho

Chi-Rho is an abbreviation of *Christ*. Chi and rho are the first two Greek letters of the word *Christ*.

 Alpha and Omega

Alpha and Omega are the first and last letters of the Greek alphabet. In the New Testament Book of Revelation, Jesus calls himself the Alpha and the Omega. He existed before anything else and will always exist. He is the First and the Last, the Beginning and the End.

Lamb of God

The lamb is a symbol of both innocence and sacrifice. The Lamb of God is an ancient symbol of the sinless, innocent Christ who shed his blood and sacrificed his life on the cross.

 Butterfly

The butterfly is a symbol of the Risen Christ. A butterfly metamorphoses from a caterpillar to a chrysalis and finally becomes a butterfly. Christ was born of Mary, was crucified and buried in a tomb, and then was raised from the dead as the glorified Christ.

Fish

The Greek letters ICHTHUS spell the Greek word for "fish." These Greek letters are also an acronym for Jesus Christ, Son of God, Savior.

 Loaves and Fishes

Each of the four Gospels contains the account of Jesus feeding the crowd with loaves of bread and fish. From the earliest days of the Church, loaves and fish have been a symbol both of Jesus, the Bread of Life, and for the Eucharist.

Think about your faith in Jesus Christ. Choose a belief of the Catholic Church about Jesus. What symbol would you create to share your faith in Jesus with others?

WHAT DIFFERENCE
Does Faith Make in My Life?

Respecting and Accepting Differences

You are a follower, or disciple, of Jesus Christ. As his disciple, you are a living symbol of Christ. When members of your family, classmates, and neighbors see you and listen to you, you are a living symbol of Christ's saving love for them. Christ works through you to bring his love, healing, understanding, and compassion to others.

Jesus treated everyone with love and respect. He accepted all people—Jewish people and Gentiles, children and adults, widows and newlyweds, soldiers and scribes, Pharisees and tax collectors. Respecting and accepting others are keys to loving one another as Jesus loves us. They are keys to being a living symbol of Christ.

Living Symbols of Christ

Being a living symbol of Christ is not always easy. You, like everyone else, need to work at respecting and accepting all people as Jesus did.

Most people find it easy to like people who seem to be somewhat like themselves. For example: Think of how much you and your friends have in common. You probably share more likes than differences. You may share interests in the same music, sports, and hobbies. You enjoy being together and just seem to get along well, at least most of the time.

Sometimes the differences people have keep them from accepting and respecting one another. For example: Others may speak a language different from yours, or the color of their skin might be different from yours. Others might not be as athletic or smart or popular as you would like them to be. Or you might not like someone because their personality clashes with yours.

Not liking *something* about a person is okay. What is not okay is ridiculing and making fun of someone because they are different from you. We all need to work at treating people with the respect they deserve. All people are children of God, created by him as unique and special persons.

How does peer pressure affect your acceptance of others?

Here are some things you can do to work on accepting others and treating everyone with the respect they deserve.

❖ Remember that each person is a child of God.
❖ Take the time to get to know the other person.
❖ Look for the goodness within each person.
❖ Treat others as you want them to treat you.
❖ Ask the Holy Spirit to be your helper and guide.

Faith Decision

• Form a small group. Work together to identify ways that students in your school treat one another with respect. Describe a situation in which students' differences might be used to leave somone out of things.

• Quietly reflect on how you can be a living symbol of Christ in your school.

This week I will work at being a clearer sign of Christ in my school. I will

_____

_____

_____

_____

_____

_____

_____.

Benedictus

Group 1:
Blessed be the Lord,
    the God of Israel;
he has come to his people
    and set them free.

Group 2:
He has raised up for us
    a mighty savior,
born of the house of his
    servant David.

Group 1:
Through his holy prophets
    he promised of old
that he would save us from
    our enemies, from the hands
    of all who hate us.

Group 2:
He promised to show mercy
    to our fathers
and to remember his
    holy covenant.

Group 1:
You, my child, shall be called
    the prophet of the Most High;
for you will go before the Lord
    to prepare his way,

Group 2:
To give his people knowledge
    of salvation by the
    forgiveness of their sins.

BASED ON LUKE 1:68–72, 73–77

FAITH VOCABULARY

Define each of these faith terms:
1. Immaculate Conception   2. Lord
3. YHWH   4. Incarnation

MAIN IDEAS

Choose either (a) or (b) from each set of items.
Write a brief paragraph to answer each of
your choices.

1. (a) Describe the unique role God chose
        for Mary in his plan of salvation.
   (b) Explain what the Catholic Church
        teaches about the mystery of the
        Incarnation.
2. (a) Describe what the Infancy Narratives
        in Matthew's and Luke's accounts of
        the Gospel teach us about the Catholic
        Church's faith in Jesus.
   (b) What do we mean by the public life,
        or public ministry, of Jesus?

CRITICAL THINKING

Using what you have learned in this chapter,
briefly explain this statement:
    In order to be a Christian, a person must
    believe that Jesus Christ is the Son of God.

FAMILY DISCUSSION

How is our family a living symbol of Christ?

For more ideas on ways
your family can live your
faith, visit the "Faith First
for Families" page at
www.FaithFirst.com. Click
on the Teen Center to check
out the latest games.

The Transfiguration of Jesus

A Scripture Story

FAITH FOCUS

What is the importance of the story of the Transfiguration?

FAITH VOCABULARY

Transfiguration   Messiah

Why do you think people stand in wonder and awe at the base of a mountain?

Mountains just seem to attract people. Year after year, millions of Americans and visitors from other countries vacation in the grandeur and peace of the Grand Canyon and Yosemite National Park.

Mountains played a very important role in the life of God's people. Throughout the Bible the sacred writers describe key events that took place on mountains.

What is one event in the story of salvation that took place on a mountain?

Mount Tabor

LORD, God of hosts, who is like you? / . . . Tabor and Hermon rejoice in your name.
PSALM 89:9, 13

Mount Hermon

Mount Sinai

Mountains in the Scriptures

Three events at the center of the history of the Israelites occurred near or on Mount Horeb. First, it is near Mount Horeb that God revealed his name, YHWH, to Moses. Second, during the Exodus, God entered the Covenant with the Israelites on Mount Horeb and revealed the Ten Commandments. Third, on this same mountain God appeared to Elijah the Prophet.

In the Gospel of Matthew, Jesus presents the Sermon on the Mount on a mountainside near the Sea of Galilee. The Sermon on the Mount is a summary of Jesus' teachings. The Ascension of Jesus occurred on the Mount of Olives. It was also on a mountain that the **Transfiguration** of Jesus took place.

The Feast of Tabernacles

Some Biblical scholars think that the event of the Transfiguration took place during the celebration of the Jewish feast of Tabernacles, or Booths. The word *tabernacle* comes from the Latin word meaning "tent."

The name *feast of Tabernacles* has two meanings. First, it recalls the booths or tents that the workers constructed in the fields during the harvest. Second, it refers to the story of Moses and the Israelites dwelling in tents as they wandered forty years in the desert, journeying from slavery in Egypt to the land promised them by God. Thanking and blessing God, the Jewish people would offer baskets of harvest fruits on this feast and recall the saving acts of God during the Exodus.

What is the significance of mountains in Sacred Scripture?

Moses and Elijah

Moses and Elijah the Prophet both play an important role in the Gospel story of the Transfiguration of Jesus. The meaning of the Hebrew name *Elijah*, "my God is YHWH," identifies the work of Elijah, who championed that only the God of the Israelites, YHWH, is the one true God. The inclusion of Moses and Elijah in the story of the Transfiguration highlights that Jesus is the final prophet in God's plan of salvation. Jesus is the final Word of God.

While on the mountain with Jesus, the disciples told him that some people thought he was Elijah, Jeremiah, or one of the other prophets who had returned to them. Jesus, turning to Peter, asked, "But who do you say that I am?" (Matthew 16:15). Peter enthusiastically responded, "You are the Messiah, the Son of the living God" (Matthew 16:16).

Messiah is a Hebrew term for *Christ*, meaning "Anointed One." The **Messiah** was the Savior that God promised he would send to free the Israelites from oppression. Jesus continued, much to the objection of Peter and the other disciples, saying that he, the Messiah, must go to Jerusalem to suffer, be killed, and on the third day be raised from the dead.

Who did Peter profess Jesus to be?

Mount Carmel

Did you Know...

The exact location of the Mount of the Transfiguration is not known. Many believe it is one of these three mountains:

Mount Carmel is one of the mountains to which Elijah fled during his ordeal with the priests of Baal. It ascends steeply to a height of 2,000 feet. Covered with thickets, it is very difficult to ascend.

Mount Tabor is isolated on a plain and rises steeply to 1,850 feet.

Mount Hermon is the highest of the three mountains. Visible from the Sea of Galilee, its summit is always snow-covered. The highest of its three peaks rises to 9,232 feet.

FAITH CONNECTION

If someone asked you, "Who is Jesus?" what would you say? Write your answer in this space.

_____

_____

_____

Reading the Word of God

The Transfiguration

On the last day of the feast of Tabernacles, Jesus took Peter, James, and John his brother up a high mountain by themselves. It was there Jesus was transfigured before them. The word *transfiguration* means "marked change in appearance, especially a change that glorifies." Matthew writes:

[Jesus'] face shone like the sun and his clothes became white as light. And behold, Moses and Elijah appeared to them, conversing with him. Then Peter said to Jesus in reply, "Lord, it is good that we are here. If you wish, I will make three tents here, one for you, one for Moses, and one for Elijah." While he was still speaking, behold, a bright cloud cast a shadow over them, then from the cloud came a voice that said, "This is my beloved Son, with whom I am well pleased; listen to him." When the disciples heard this, they fell prostrate and were very much afraid. But Jesus came and touched them, saying, "Rise, and do not be afraid." And when the disciples raised their eyes, they saw no one else but Jesus alone.

As they were coming down from the mountain, Jesus charged them, "Do not tell the vision to anyone until the Son of Man has been raised from the dead." Then the disciples asked him, "Why do the scribes say that Elijah must come first?" He said in reply, "Elijah will indeed come and restore all things; but I tell you that Elijah has already come, and they did not recognize him but did to him whatever they pleased. So also will the Son of Man suffer at their hands." Then the disciples understood that he was speaking to them of John the Baptist.   MATTHEW 17:2–13

The Transfiguration.
James J. Tissot
(1836–1902), French artist

Something amazing occurred on the mountain. The Apostles Peter, James, and John were astounded. One moment Jesus was as they knew him; the next he appeared very different; then he was the same again.

Jesus' appearance changed so incredibly that Matthew the Evangelist has to compare Jesus' transfigured appearance to a powerful natural phenomenon: Jesus' face became bright "like the sun and his clothes became white as light" (Matthew 17:2).

How can a knowledge of Moses, Elijah, Jeremiah, and the other Old Testament prophets help you understand the meaning of the Transfiguration?

Contemporary Transfiguration scene, *Vie de Jesus Mafa*.

The Identity of Jesus

The Transfiguration clarifies the identity of Jesus and the meaning of his work, or ministry, on earth. Jesus is the Incarnate Son of God, who fulfilled the Law of Moses and the Prophets.

Moses and Elijah

The inclusion of Moses and of Elijah is symbolic of the Law (delivered by Moses) and the Prophets (symbolized by Elijah). These two pillars upon which Jewish tradition is based are brought to fulfillment in Jesus Christ, the new and everlasting Covenant.

Why is Elijah included in the event of the Transfiguration?

A Voice from Heaven

At the voice from heaven the disciples were overcome with "fear"—a reverential fear, a sense of wonder and awe, in the presence of God, who is all holy. The disciples were to listen to Jesus, the Word of God.

Jesus' Passion and Death

The work of salvation the Father sent Jesus to do would bring him to Jerusalem. There Jesus, the Savior of the world, would be arrested and tried, suffer and be crucified upon the cross, buried and raised from the dead. At the Transfiguration Peter, James, and John were given a glimpse into the meaning of that suffering. After witnessing the Transfiguration, the disciples came to know and believe that suffering and death were the way to Jesus' future glory. This faith would sustain the disciples and the readers of Matthew in the dark days ahead.

FAITH : CONNECTION

Describe a situation in your life that looking at it with eyes of faith, made all the difference.

_____

_____

_____

_____

OUR CHURCH
MAKES A DIFFERENCE

Blessed Mother Teresa of Calcutta

Blessed Mother Teresa of Calcutta (1910–1997) saw everyone and everything through the eyes of faith. She dedicated the last forty years of her life to ministering with those who were destitute and suffering and dying and abandoned on the streets of Calcutta, India.

Blessed Mother Teresa made such a difference in the world that in 1979 she was awarded the Nobel Prize for Peace. In 1996 she became the fourth person ever to be nominated as an honorary citizen of America. The entire world mourned Mother Teresa's death on September 5, 1997. On October 19, 2003, Pope John Paul II beatified, or named her, Blessed Mother Teresa.

What member of the Church has inspired you to see people and events with the eyes of faith?

Sisters of the Missionaries of Charity at tomb of Blessed Mother Teresa, their founder

WHAT DIFFERENCE
Does Faith Make in My Life?

Seeing with Eyes of Faith

The events that the Apostles Peter, James, and John experienced at the Transfiguration changed the way they looked at things. You are blessed with the grace to see people, places, and events with the eyes of faith.

Here are some skills you can practice to help you see things differently. Using these skills will help you move beyond the first impressions you may have of people, places, and events. These skills will sharpen your vision. They will help you place your expectations aside; they will help you look for the deeper meaning of things. They will help you see God present in your life and in the lives of others.

1. **Take some time.**
   Look more closely and see beyond the surface. At first glance, a person or a situation may be easily misinterpreted.

2. **Take off your mask.**
   Do not put on airs or pretend to be something or someone else. Let people really get to know you, and you will find out they can really like you. Try always to be yourself. Remember, an original is better than a copy. There is no one else quite like you. You truly are unique and special.

3. **Get to know the person.**
   Be willing to give someone a chance to share who they really are. Sometimes people are afraid to let you know who they really are because you may laugh at them or not like them or accept them.

4. **Ask questions.**
   Clarify the situation. Sometimes things are not what they seem. People are not always who they appear to be. Some people put on masks and pretend to be tough or aloof or not friendly.

5. **Do not judge.**
   See the goodness within people. Jesus warned us against judging other people. He said, "Stop judging, that you may not be judged" (Matthew 7:1). Treat others the way you would like them to treat you. Remember, we are all God's children.

Faith · Decision

- Describe a situation where you learned more information and gained new insights by getting to know someone better. Create a profile of the person. Write or draw what you now know about the person.

- Form a small group. Discuss ways you can see things with the eyes of faith by practicing one of the above skills.

This week I will try to see with the eyes of faith by

_____

_____

_____

_____

_____

_____

The Gloria

All:
Glory to God in the highest,
and on earth peace
   to people of good will.

Leader:
We praise you, we bless you,
we adore you, we glorify you,
we give you thanks for
   your great glory,
Lord God, heavenly King,
O God, almighty Father.

All:
Glory to God in the highest.

Leader:
Lord Jesus Christ,
   Only Begotten Son,
Lord God, Lamb of God,
Son of the Father, you take
   away the sins of the world,
   have mercy on us;
you take away the sins of the
world, receive our prayer;
you are seated at the right
   hand of the Father,
   have mercy on us.

All:
Glory to God in the highest.

Leader:
For you alone are the Holy One,
you alone are the Lord,
you alone are the Most High,
Jesus Christ,
   with the Holy Spirit,
   in the glory of God the
   Father. Amen.

All:
Glory to God in the highest,
and on earth peace
   to people of good will.

FAITH VOCABULARY

Define each of these faith terms:
1. Transfiguration   2. Messiah

MAIN IDEAS

Choose either (a) or (b) from each set of items. Write a paragraph to answer each of your choices.

1. (a) Explain the importance of mountains in the events of God's people.
   (b) Describe what the presence of Moses and Elijah at the Transfiguration tells us about the meaning of this event.

2. (a) Explain the significance of the voice from heaven in the Transfiguration story.
   (b) Describe the main message of the event of the Transfiguration.

CRITICAL THINKING

Using what you have learned in this chapter, briefly explain this statement:
   When we see people, places, and events in our lives through the eyes of faith, they are "transfigured" before our eyes.

FAMILY DISCUSSION

How might seeing the members of our family with eyes of faith make a difference in how we treat one another?

For more ideas on ways your family can live your faith, visit the "Faith First for Families" page at **www.FaithFirst.com**. Also check out the Teen Center for additional activities.

The Suffering Servant

A Scripture Story

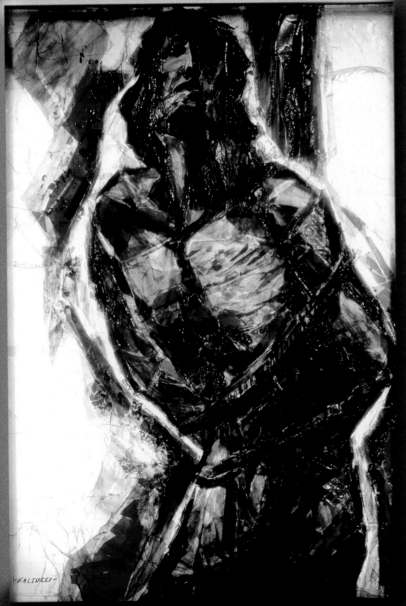

Crucifixion. Falucci

How do the writings of Isaiah help us understand the work of Jesus?

prophets   suffering Servant

When have you ever been asked to deliver a message to someone? How important was it for you to deliver the message correctly and on time?

People get messages all the time. Delivering messages and delivering them safely and on time is so important that today companies have been formed just for that purpose.

The Bible is filled with people whom God chose to deliver his message to his people. Among these messengers the **prophets** have an important place. The word *prophet* comes from a Greek word that means "one who speaks before others."

In what way could we say that Jesus was a prophet?

Son though he was, he learned obedience from what he suffered; and when he was made perfect, he became the source of eternal salvation for all who obey him.
HEBREWS 5:8–9

Isaiah

Isaiah the Prophet

The Old Testament prophets brought many varied messages to the people from God. Many prophets, such as Jeremiah, often denounced God's people for abandoning the Covenant and placing their trust and faith in the false gods their neighbors worshiped and honored.

Other prophets, such as Amos, condemned injustice. They reminded God's people of their obligation and responsibility to care for one another—especially the poor and widowed.

Still other prophets, such as Isaiah, delivered messages of hope to God's people during times of suffering and persecution. Isaiah lived and worked in the city of Jerusalem between 742 B.C. and 701 B.C. during the time of the Assyrian conquest of western Asia. He was married and had two sons, and probably came from an aristocratic family. The message of Isaiah to God's people is perhaps clearly summarized in the very meaning of the name Isaiah, which is "YHWH is salvation."

Of all the writings of the Old Testament prophets, the Book of Isaiah is named most often in the New Testament. It is referred to thirteen times in the accounts of the Gospel, three times in the Acts of the Apostles, and six times in the Letter to the Romans.

By the Waters of Babylon. James J. Tissot (1836–1902), French artist

The writings of the prophets are contained in the prophetic books of the Old Testament. Tradition has classified the writings of the prophets into the major prophets and the minor prophets. This classification is based on the length of the Old Testament books. The writings of eighteen prophets are included in the Catholic Bible. They are:

- the major prophets Isaiah, Ezekiel, and Jeremiah;
- the minor prophets Hosea, Joel, Amos, Obadiah, Jonah, Micah, Nahum, Habakkuk, Zephaniah, Haggai, Zechariah, and Malachi;
- the Book of Baruch, the Book of Lamentations, and the Book of Daniel.

The Book of Isaiah

The Book of Isaiah has sixty-six chapters, which are divided into three parts: chapters 1–39, chapters 40–55, and chapters 56–66. The second part of the book contains four poems, or songs, called servant songs. These passages focus on a figure called the "Servant of YHWH." The best known of these images of the Servant of YHWH is that of the **suffering Servant.**

The suffering Servant was probably not a specific person but rather the idealization, or ideal or perfect image, of the faithful Jew suffering in exile whose life was an offering for the sins of the nations. The suffering of the Jewish people in their exile in Babylon would serve as a light to the nations. When the Jewish people were freed from exile, other nations would acknowledge YHWH as the one true God.

The second part of the Book of Isaiah was also written to celebrate God's promise to free the Jews from exile. In this part of his writings the prophet encouraged the people in their huge task of rebuilding the nation of Israel.

Why do you think the image of the suffering Servant was helpful to the Jewish people during the exile?

FAITH CONNECTION

Write a message for a bumper sticker that delivers a Christian message of hope to people.

_____

_____

_____

Jesus accepts his cross.

Jesus falls the first time.

Jesus meets his mother.

The Sinless Servant

The last of the four servant songs gives an extraordinary description of a sinless servant who by his voluntary suffering atones for the sins of his people. In this fourth servant song we read:

See, my servant shall prosper,
    he shall be raised high and
        greatly exalted.
Even as many were amazed
    at him—
    so marred was his look beyond
        that of man,
    and his appearance beyond
        that of mortals—
So shall he startle many nations,
    because of him kings shall
        stand speechless;

For those who have not been told
    shall see,
those who have not heard shall
    ponder it.

Who would believe what we have
    heard?
To whom has the arm of the
    LORD been revealed?
He grew up like a sapling
    before him,
    like a shoot from the parched
        earth;
There was in him no stately
    bearing to make us look
        at him,
    nor appearance that would
        attract us to him.

ISAIAH 52:13–15; 53:1–2

Simon helps Jesus carry his cross.

Jesus is nailed to the cross.

Jesus is taken down from the cross.

He was spurned and avoided
    by men,
    a man of suffering, accustomed
    to infirmity,
One of those from whom men
    hide their faces,
    spurned, and we held him in
    no esteem.

Like a lamb led to the slaughter
    or a sheep before the shearers,
    he was silent and opened not
    his mouth.
Oppressed and condemned, he
    was taken away,
    and who would have thought
    any more of his destiny? . . .

Through his suffering, my servant
    shall justify many,
    and their guilt he shall bear. . . .
And he shall take away the sins
    of many,
    and win pardon for their
    offenses.   ISAIAH 53:3, 7–8, 11–12

Jesus' first disciples were Jews
who would have been very familiar
with the writings of Isaiah the
Prophet. Reflecting on this passage,
they came to believe that this
prophecy of Isaiah was fulfilled in
Jesus Christ, who suffered and shed
his blood "on behalf of many for the
forgiveness of sins" (Matthew 26:28).

**Compare the suffering of the suffering
Servant with the suffering of Jesus.**

87

those of Christ, were making a difference. Their suffering had meaning and value for their own salvation and the salvation of the world.

How did the prophecy of Isaiah help the early Church understand Jesus?

Good Friday

The celebration of Good Friday helps us connect the sufferings of Christ with our own life in Christ. As Christians our suffering and pain are signs of Christ's suffering and pain. The Liturgy of Good Friday proclaims the great mystery of our faith—by the death of Jesus, we are freed from death and receive the promise of eternal life.

The Good Friday liturgy helps open our eyes to see what Jesus did for us—and for all people. Through hearing and reflecting on the Scripture readings proclaimed on that day, we hear that Jesus freely suffered and gave his life for us. Our veneration of the cross on Good Friday is a tangible sign of our deep gratitude and love for Jesus Christ, who suffered, died, and gave his life for us.

The Suffering Church

Jesus, the sinless, suffering Servant of God, suffered voluntarily to atone for the sins of all people. The Passion and death of Jesus, the suffering Servant, saved all the people from just punishment from God.

Christians quickly came to understand that they, as Jesus did, would suffer. Joined to Christ in Baptism, Christians recognized that their pains and suffering, joined to

FAITH CONNECTION

What prayers or thoughts help you deal with suffering?

_____

_____

_____

_____

OUR CHURCH
MAKES A DIFFERENCE

Archbishop Helder Camara

There are some people who bring us comfort and hope when we are suffering. Archbishop Helder Camara of Brazil did just that. In Christ's name he was a champion for human rights and a defender of the poor. Most people knew Archbishop Camara by the simple title of "Dom Helder." He died on August 27, 1999, at the age of ninety-two.

When he was a young priest in Rio de Janeiro, Dom Helder ministered with many people who were living in substandard housing, were underfed, and went without medical care. When Dom Helder became Archbishop of Olinda and Recife in Brazil in 1964, he chose to live the remaining thirty-five years of his life in one room behind the Church of the Frontiers in Olinda. This simple room was furnished with only a sink, a stove, a table, and a hammock that he used as his bed.

Dom Helder constantly spoke out for the poor and against the many violations of the human rights of the poor—especially their torture—which the government security forces practiced. This so angered the Brazilian government that its officials pressured the news media never to mention his name.

The Year 2000 Poverty Campaign, which Dom Helder launched in 1990, is an international campaign to eradicate and diminish poverty among the world's poorest people. The Campaign, built on the Gospel teaching that we are all children of the same Father, strives to reach the goal of helping all people fulfill their basic human needs for survival.

Where do you see people suffering in your community? Who reaches out to share comfort and hope with them?

WHAT DIFFERENCE
Does Faith Make in My Life?

Dealing with Loss

During his life on earth Jesus showed us how to deal with suffering, both physical and emotional. Thinking about the life of Jesus helps us deal not only with the suffering, both great and small, that comes about from loss, but also with death.

Here are some common losses, big and small. Look over the list. Check the losses you have experienced.

____ confidence
____ a friend
____ a parent through divorce
____ a parent or a loved one
through death
____ missing the honor roll
____ an arm or a leg
____ health
____ a game
____ not making the team
____ money or your bike
____ your family pet
____ your home due to fire, flood,
hurricane, or tornado
____ other: _____
_____

A loss of any kind stirs up feelings and emotions within us. The deeper the loss, the deeper the pain and suffering may be. When you suffer a loss, you may feel sad, mad, hurt, shocked, disappointed, defeated, depressed, lonely, scared, guilty, or rejected. You may experience some of these feelings intensely.

How you choose to handle your experiences of loss and the emotions that accompany them makes all the difference. You can choose a positive way to deal with your emotions or a negative way of staying trapped in these feelings. You can choose to avoid the feelings and pretend they do not bother you, but they will keep surfacing until you deal with what happened to you. Whatever emotions you may feel are real. Remember, feelings are not bad or good; they just are. Choose to deal positively with what you feel and you can heal.

As Christians we believe that good will triumph over evil. By Jesus' suffering and death on the cross and his Resurrection to new life, he has saved us and has given us the gift of hope. Hope makes all the difference. Hope helps us change and grow stronger as we work through our suffering and loss. Our Christian hope means we believe and trust that God will never abandon us, and we will enjoy eternal life with God forever.

HOPE means we live with an
    Honest,
    Optimistic,
    Persistent,
    Effort to **H**andle **O**ur **P**ainful
      Emotions and attain
    Heaven, **O**ur **P**romise of **E**ternity.

Faith · Decision

- In a small group or with a partner share one of the losses you checked on page 90. Discuss how the gift of hope has helped you deal with the situation.

- Name a person who is a role model for you or an example of how to deal with suffering and loss.

Christians are people of hope. The Resurrection is the pledge of our own resurrection and life everlasting. This week I can be a living sign of hope. I will

_____

_____

_____.

PRAY and REVIEW

Veneration of the Cross

Leader:
We adore you, O Christ,
and we bless you,

All:
Because by your holy cross
you have redeemed the world.

Reader:
A reading from the letter
to the Hebrews.
(Read Hebrews 4:14–16, 5:7–9.)
The word of the Lord.

All:
Thanks be to God.
(Step forward and venerate
the cross of Christ.)

Leader:
Heavenly Father,
by the suffering of your Son,
Jesus Christ,
you have saved us all from
the power of sin and death.
In your goodness, make us
holy and give us the grace
to live in the hope of the
resurrection and the life
everlasting.
We ask this through Christ
our Lord.

All: Amen.

FAITH VOCABULARY

Define each of these faith terms:

1. prophets
2. suffering Servant

MAIN IDEAS

Choose either (a) or (b) from each set of items.
Write a brief paragraph to answer each of
your choices.

1. (a) Describe the role and message of the
Old Testament prophets.
   (b) What are the servant songs found in
the Book of Isaiah?

2. (a) What are some of the images found in
the fourth servant song in the Book of
Isaiah?
   (b) Describe the way the early Church
explained the servant songs.

CRITICAL THINKING

Using what you have learned in this chapter,
briefly explain how the fourth servant song
helps us understand the Paschal Mystery of
Jesus Christ.

FAMILY DISCUSSION

In times of loss and suffering, how can we
support one another?

For more ideas on ways your
family can live your faith, visit the
"Faith First for Families" page at
www.FaithFirst.com. Also visit
the Teen Center and check
out the "Make a Difference"
activity for this week.

Jesus' Passion and Death

9

What works of art do you know that have been inspired by the life and work of Jesus?

Many of the world's greatest artists, composers, poets, and playwrights have found inspiration for creating their works in the story of Jesus Christ. Jesus was God's chosen instrument to make "all things work for good" (Romans 8:28). Everything about him—his silences, his miracles, his gestures, his approach to individuals, his prayer, his genuine affection for people, his special care for the vulnerable and the poor—teach us about God's love at work in our lives, especially in the most difficult of times when evil seems to threaten us.

How does the life, work, and Person of Jesus inspire you?

[Jesus said,] "It is finished." And bowing his head, he handed over the spirit.
JOHN 19:30

Jesus: The New Adam

Adam and Eve being cast out of the Garden of Eden

God created Adam and Eve in his own image. He set them over the whole world to serve him and to care for all creatures. Adam and Eve were so free, in fact, that they could even turn their back on God and choose to go their own way. Sadly for the human race, they did just that.

The Book of Genesis describes how Satan, the serpent-tempter, lured Adam and Eve to test the limits of their freedom. Satan enticed them to eat from "the tree of knowledge of good and bad" (Genesis 2:17), which symbolized the temptation to become like God. Adam and Eve gave in to this temptation.

Original Justice

Prior to the Incarnation the pages of Sacred Scripture paint a troubling picture. The problems began with Adam and Eve, from whom the whole human race can trace their common origin. This chosen couple had everything going for them. The world was filled with abundance. Everything was in harmony with God. Justice and order prevailed. Death was unheard of. The term to describe this initial, or original, condition of human life is *original justice*, or original holiness.

Original Sin

Adam and Eve's choice of evil over good, of doing their own thing over obeying God, is called **original sin.** As a result of original sin, which "is transmitted with human nature" (see *Catechism of the Catholic Church* 419), human nature is weakened.

Instead of an inheritance of harmony and unity with God, this misguided couple left us a legacy of wars, destruction, injustice, murders, prejudice, anger, envy, greed, guilt, and the possibility of eternal separation from God after death.

What are some of the effects of original sin that you see in the world today?

The Problem of Evil

The suffering, death, and evil in the world are the result of original sin. They were not part of God's plan for creation. They resulted from the misuse of the gift of freedom and free choice that God gave to Adam and Eve and gives to every person.

Moral evil is linked to the mystery of the gift of human freedom. It is the harm we willingly inflict on one another and on God's good creation. God is in no way, directly or even indirectly, the cause of moral evil.

From the greatest evil, the Crucifixion of Jesus, and from the greatest loving use of freedom, Jesus freely sacrificing his life on the cross, God brought about the greatest of goods: Christ's Resurrection and our **Redemption.** *Redemption* is the word we use to describe Christ delivering us from sin and death through the **Paschal Mystery** of his Passion, death, Resurrection, and glorious Ascension (see Acts of the Apostles 4:12).

How does the Paschal Mystery of Christ illustrate good coming out of evil?

Did you Know...

The Church makes a distinction between moral evil and physical evil. Physical evil refers to sickness and illness and to such destructive forces of nature as hurricanes, tornadoes, raging flood waters, mud slides, drought, and so on. "The fact that God permits physical and even moral evil is a mystery that God illuminates by his Son Jesus Christ who died and rose to vanquish evil. Faith gives us the certainty that God would not permit an evil if he did not cause a good to come from that very evil, by ways that we shall fully know only in eternal life" (*Catechism of the Catholic Church*, 324).

FAITH CONNECTION

Describe an "evil" situation you have experienced, have read about, or have seen reported, in which you discovered something good.

_____

_____

_____

_____

_____

Jesus: The New Adam

God did not stand by idly after Adam sinned. He promised that the divine plan of creation would be repaired. Life would be victorious over death, and justice and holiness over sin (see Genesis 3:15). The Old Testament is a testimony to God's efforts to save humanity from sin and his continuing invitation to humanity to turn their lives over to his divine care.

The time finally came for God to send forth the One who would repair the damage. God the Father sent his Son. In Jesus, the Incarnate Son of God, the divine plan of salvation was fulfilled.

Jesus is the new Adam (see 1 Corinthians 15:20–28). By freely choosing to give up his life in obedience to God's will, Jesus has given us even greater blessings than those that Adam's sin had taken from us.

Explain why Jesus is the new Adam.

Jesus' Cross/Our Crosses

The Son of God became a man to save us from our sins. The Father anointed Christ (that title, in fact, means "Anointed One") with the Holy Spirit to save us from the power of sin and death and to make amends for our sins. This is why we say that Jesus' death on the cross was an **expiation** for our sins.

Expiation heals a broken relationship. Jesus paid the price for all the evils men and women produce. He made amends for all the harm we willingly inflict on one another.

Evil happens today in all of our lives. Evil—such as being ridiculed at school, violence, injustices, betrayal by friends, harassment, and gossip—catches up with us and hoists us up on our own bitterly painful crosses. Jesus invited his disciples to take up their crosses and follow him (see Matthew 16:24). When we suffer, we join our sufferings with Christ's. In some way, known only to God, Jesus also suffers with us.

Name some of the crosses that people have to carry today.

The Death of Jesus

On May 28, 1888, an amateur photographer snapped a picture of a shroud, or burial cloth, that showed what many believed to be an image of the body of Jesus. This shroud, the Shroud of Turin, is believed by many to be the cloth that wrapped Jesus' body for burial. The Church has not officially declared the Shroud of Turin to be Jesus' burial cloth, but the shroud remains an image that awakens deep faith.

The Gospels describe Jesus' death by crucifixion. Historical records support what the Gospel says. Crucifixion was used as a means of execution. It was intended to deter others from rebelling against the power of the Roman state.

Jesus Truly Died

Jesus truly died a real, physical death and entered the dwelling place of the dead. From the time that he died on the cross until his Resurrection, he experienced the condition of death—separation of his soul from his body.

The Gospel meticulously describes that Jesus was taken down from the cross and buried in a nearby tomb (see John 19:38–42). There is no reason to think that Jesus merely pretended to be dead. Scripture tells us that by the grace of God he tasted death for everyone (see Hebrews 2:9).

Why is the historical fact of Jesus' death so important to Christians?

Did you Know...

A wonderfully poetic, ancient homily read in the Liturgy of the Hours on Holy Saturday captures the meaning of Jesus' descent to the regions of the dead:

Today a great silence reigns upon earth,
a great silence and a great stillness.
A great silence because the king is asleep.
The earth trembled and is still because God has fallen asleep in the flesh and he has raised up all who have slept ever since the world began. . . .
He has gone to search for Adam, our first father, as for a lost sheep. . . .
"I order you, O sleeper, to awake.
I did not create you to be a prisoner in hell.
Rise from the dead, for I am the life of the dead."

Descent to the Dead

Every time we pray the Apostles' Creed we say:

[He] suffered under Pontius Pilate,
was crucified, died,
and was buried;
he descended into hell; . . .

After Jesus died but before he was raised from the dead, Jesus descended to the dead, the place where the souls of the dead live separated from God. Actually, what confuses us about this event is the word *hell*, which is used in the praying of the Apostles' Creed, a place generally associated with damnation and endless suffering. The word *hell* in this instance is used for the Hebrew word *sheol*, which simply means "the abode of the dead."

Upon his death, Jesus entered sheol, where he joined the souls of all who had preceded him in death. The First Letter of Peter teaches, "[T]he gospel was preached even to the dead" (1 Peter 4:6).

Christ's descent to the dead vividly demonstrates his love for and sensitivity to all people. His first act after death was to reunite himself with those who had already died. Imagine the intense joy felt by these just women and men who had gone before him as he opened heaven's gates for them to enter.

Jesus' death made amends for the sins of humankind. It reconciled human beings with God. From his descent to the dead we learn that God does not wish to exclude anyone from his kingdom. Christ is the Savior of all people.

Detail from *Descent into Hell*, fifteenth-century Russian icon

FAITH : CONNECTION

How does the fact that Jesus died help you understand better the meaning of the death of someone?

_____

_____

_____

Stations of the Cross

Catholics profess their faith in the meaning of the Crucifixion for their lives by praying the Stations, or Way, of the Cross. Making the Stations of the Cross is a small pilgrimage. A pilgrimage is a spiritual journey to a specific place to remember a special event that occurred there.

Pilgrimages to the Holy Land became very popular in the Middle Ages. In 1342 the Franciscans took over the care of the shrines in the Holy Land. They promoted a great devotion to these sacred places. Since the number of Christians who were able to visit the Holy Land was very limited, shrines, or stations, commemorating the important events in the life of Jesus— especially his Passion and death—were placed in local churches.

Saint Leonard of Port Maurice (1676–1751), a Franciscan, set up more than 572 sets of the Stations of the Cross and became known as the "preacher of the Stations of the Cross." The most famous place he set up the Stations of the Cross is in the Colosseum of Rome. Each year during Holy Week, the pope joins with Christian pilgrims and prays the Stations of the Cross there.

Popular custom has set the number of stations, or stops, on the Way of the Cross at fourteen. Today a fifteenth station, the Resurrection, is often added to emphasize that the Passion and death of Christ *and* the Resurrection "have set us free."

How does your parish help you "walk through" the Passion, death, and Resurrection of Jesus during Holy Week?

Pope John Paul II preaching at the Colosseum on Good Friday

WHAT DIFFERENCE
Does Faith Make in My Life?

From Sadness to Hope

Jesus' Passion and death was a time of pain and grief for Jesus' followers. You can imagine how especially difficult it must have been for his mother, Mary, to see her Son suffer and die.

Sadness and death are in some way a part of everyone's life. When someone you love dies, you may be filled with deep feelings of grief and experience a time of sorrow.

Death is the doorway to new and eternal life with God. In the funeral liturgy we celebrate not only the ending of a life but the beginning of a person's eternal life. This truth of faith gives us hope to deal with grief.

What Can You Do?

There are some things that will help you as you move through the grieving process.

1. **Pray.**
   Remember that God loves you and is always with you. Ask the Holy Spirit to give you hope and strength. Pray to your loved one to help you handle the feelings you are experiencing.

2. Have hope.
Remember Jesus' promise and have hope. He said, "In my Father's house there are many dwelling places. . . . And if I go and prepare a place for you, I will come back again and take you to myself, so that where I am you also may be" (John 14:2–3). Feelings of sadness and grief can be like waves rolling over you. Sometimes they can knock you down.

3. Keep a journal.
Write a letter to the person who has died and share what is in your heart. You can then put the letter in a special place. Writing letters can help you express your emotions and feel a little bit better.

4. Process your grief.
Work through your grieving. Grieving is a process. Healing takes as long as it takes. Be aware that the Lord Jesus is present with you. There is no limit on how long he is with you, reaching out to help you heal.

5. Express your feelings.
Share your feelings with those you love, especially with God. It is healthy. It is not a sign of weakness but a sign of strength.

Faith Decision

- Name the feelings that may accompany the grieving process.

- Some people use colors to express how they feel. For example, gray may depict feelings of sadness. Think of a particular grieving situation you have experienced. Use color to express how you feel. Draw and share your picture with a partner.

This week I will think about God's promise of everlasting life. This will help me to

_____

_____

_____ .

PRAY and REVIEW

Litany of the Holy Name of Jesus

Leader: Jesus, Son of the living God
All: have mercy on us.

Leader: Jesus, king of glory
All: have mercy on us.

Leader: Jesus, dawn of justice
All: have mercy on us.

Leader: Jesus, pattern of patience
All: have mercy on us.

Leader: Jesus, model of obedience
All: have mercy on us.

Leader: Jesus, our refuge
All: have mercy on us.

Leader: Jesus, Good Shepherd
All: have mercy on us.

Leader: Jesus, our way and our life
All: have mercy on us.

Leader: Jesus, courage of martyrs
All: have mercy on us.

Leader: Jesus, crown of all saints
All: have mercy on us.

FAITH VOCABULARY

Define each of these faith terms:

1. original sin
2. Redemption
3. expiation
4. Paschal Mystery

MAIN IDEAS

Choose either (a) or (b) from each set of items. Write a brief paragraph to answer each of your choices.

1. (a) Describe the effects of original sin.
   (b) Why does the Church identify Jesus as the new Adam?

2. (a) Describe the connection between the mystery of moral evil in the world and the suffering and death of Jesus.
   (b) How does Jesus' suffering and death help us deal with the crosses in our own lives?

CRITICAL THINKING

Using what you have learned in this chapter, briefly explain this statement:
God can make "all things work for good."

FAMILY DISCUSSION

What crosses has our family had to bear? How has the gift of hope helped us to cope with and understand those difficult times?

For more ideas on ways your family can live your faith, visit the "Faith First for Families" page at **www.FaithFirst.com**. Also remember to read the next chapter of "Vista Falls Junior High" on the Teen Center.

Jesus' Resurrection and Ascension

FAITH FOCUS

Why is Jesus' Resurrection and Ascension our greatest source of hope?

FAITH VOCABULARY

Resurrection

Ascension

heaven

Last Judgment

purgatory

hell

What is the most dramatic event you have experienced? What made it so important?

The news sometimes reports dramatic and life-changing events. Three days after Jesus' Crucifixion, his disciples were proclaiming, "Jesus is risen! Jesus is risen!" Jesus' Resurrection changed their lives. No other event in human history has ever changed the lives of people more than the Resurrection.

Why is the Resurrection the cornerstone of Christian faith?

Easter Vigil, Procession during the Service of Light

[I]f Christ has not been raised, your faith is in vain.
1 Corinthians 15:17

Jesus' Resurrection and Ascension

"Jesus Is Risen"

The mystery of Jesus' **Resurrection** from the dead resides at the heart of faith in Christ. The Resurrection is Jesus' being raised from the dead to a new, glorified life. It is the "bodily rising of Jesus from the dead on the third day after his death on the cross and burial in the tomb" (see *Catechism of the Catholic Church*, "Glossary"). It is the reuniting of his human self to a new and glorified body. It is the source of our hope in our own resurrection that we profess in faith in the creed.

The Risen Christ

The Resurrection of Jesus is a real event. History records the event through the testimony of those who saw, talked to, walked with, and ate with the Risen, glorified Christ. Around the year 56, Saint Paul the Apostle testified:

> For I handed on to you as of first importance what I also received: that Christ died for our sins in accordance with the scriptures; that he was buried; that he was raised on the third day in accordance with the scriptures; that he appeared to Cephas [Peter], then to the Twelve. After that, he appeared to more than five hundred brothers at once, most of whom are still living.
>
> 1 CORINTHIANS 15:3–6

The Resurrection is a true mystery of our faith. It is the work of the Trinity. All three divine Persons act together to effect Jesus' history-shattering Easter miracle. The Father's power "raised up" Jesus. By so doing, the glorified Son's humanity is brought into the life of the Trinity. Once raised from the dead, the glorified Son of God joins with the Father to send, as promised, the gift of the Advocate, the Holy Spirit, to his disciples.

The Gospel accounts, as well as the Acts of the Apostles and other New Testament letters, name those who met firsthand with the Risen Christ. Despite the efforts of nonbelievers since that first Easter Sunday to discredit these witnesses and their testimony, the authenticity of that testimony is simply a matter of record.

Why is the Resurrection the crowning truth of our faith in Christ?

Jesus Returns to His Father

Forty days after the Resurrection, Jesus met with his disciples on a mountain in Galilee. Here is what happened:

> [A]s they [the apostles] were looking on, he was lifted up, and a cloud took him from their sight. While they were looking intently at the sky as he was going, suddenly two men dressed in white garments stood beside them. They said, "Men of Galilee, why are you standing there looking at the sky? This Jesus who has been taken up from you into heaven will return in the same way as you have seen him going into heaven."
>
> ACTS OF THE APOSTLES 1:9–11

We call the return of the Risen Christ to his Father, to the world of the divine, the **Ascension.**

In John Maesfield's *The Trial of Jesus*, the following fictional conversation takes place between a soldier who stood guard at Jesus' cross and the wife of Pontius Pilate. Pilate was the Roman leader who handed Jesus over to be crucified.

"Do you think he is dead?"

"No, lady, I don't."

"Then where is he?"

"Let loose in the world, lady, where . . . [no one] can stop his truth."

This was one writer's testimony to the meaning of the Ascension. The Risen Christ now glorified is at work in the world.

FAITH ⦂ CONNECTION

Create an Internet announcement proclaiming the Resurrection and Ascension of Jesus.

_____

_____

_____

The New Jerusalem, fabric Art

Jesus Is with Us

The Risen Jesus remained for forty days, during which he ate and drank with his disciples and taught them about the kingdom of God. After this time, a "cloud took him from their sight" (Acts of the Apostles 1:9). By ascending to the Father, Jesus accomplishes many things for us.

The Arrival of the Holy Spirit

Jesus' return to his Father is a necessary prelude to the sending of the Holy Spirit. The Holy Spirit is now with us as the Advocate and Teacher. He is available to us anywhere, anytime.

Access to the "Father's house" (John 14:2)

By going before us, Jesus has opened up for us the way to eternal life and happiness with God. His Ascension strengthens our hope that where he has gone, there we will follow.

Intercession on Our Behalf

The Risen, glorified Christ intercedes on our behalf. Jesus takes his place beside his Father, "that he might now appear before God on our behalf" (Hebrews 9:24).

Inauguration of a New Age

Jesus' Ascension signifies that the kingdom that he preached during his earthly ministry truly has begun. Despite all the discord and conflict we see occurring on the world's stage, his kingdom is taking hold and "will have no end" (Nicene Creed).

We might have preferred that the Risen Christ had stayed around on earth for all to see and listen to forever. The truth is that he is present with us. Before his Ascension he promised, "And behold, I am with you always, until the end of the age" (Matthew 28:20).

Explain the significance of the Ascension in God's plan for humanity.

Life Is Changed, Not Ended!

What will become of us when we die? Christians have found the answer to the mystery of human death in the Paschal Mystery of Christ. At death, life is not ended but changed!

When you take part in the celebration of the Catholic funeral liturgy, you will hear the words "Life is changed, not ended" (Preface, Christian Death I). This expresses both our hope and our faith in the meaning of the death-Resurrection-Ascension of Jesus for our life. When we die, our lives change rather than end. Jesus says it best:

"[W]hoever believes in me, even if he dies, will live, and everyone who lives and believes in me will never die." JOHN 11:25–26

At death our souls separate from our bodies. At the moment of our death Jesus will assign our souls to their final destiny. We call this our **particular judgment**, or individual judgment. The basis of this assignment, or judgment, is based on what we have done in our lives.

At the particular judgment we receive either
- **heaven**—eternal life and happiness with God and the saints forever,
- **purgatory**—an opportunity to purify and strengthen our love for God before we enter heaven, or
- **hell**—the immediate and everlasting separation from God and the saints.

Describe the Catholic teaching on life after death.

Life after Death

Sacred Scripture and Sacred Tradition give us many insights into understanding the mystery surrounding the nature of our life after death.

Rite of Final
Commendation,
Funeral Liturgy

Life Everlasting

Jesus' Resurrection and Ascension to the Father is a sign that we also will live forever. Jesus passed from death into another state, a new and glorified life beyond space and time.

Jesus is the source and principle of our resurrection. He is God's promise that we too will pass into a state beyond space and time where we will never die again. At the resurrection on the last day, the souls of everyone who ever lived will be reunited with their bodies (see 1 Corinthians 15:35–51). This resurrection of all the dead, of both the just and the unjust (see Acts of the Apostles 24:15), will precede the **Last Judgment.**

The Last Judgment is the judgment at which all humans will appear in their own resurrected bodies and give an account of their deeds, and Christ will show his identity with the least of his brothers and sisters (see Matthew 25:31–46). On that last day, Christ will reveal himself as the Lord of history. God's loving plan of goodness for his creatures will be re-created and restored. The kingdom of God will come in all its glory. Those who had accepted God's grace, who had cared for Christ in the person of his "little ones," will reign with him forever.

God will transform the cosmos into a realm of justice and peace. In this new heaven and earth there will be no more tears, suffering, and death (see Revelation 21:1–4).

FAITH : CONNECTION

What steps can you take to build a world of justice and peace?

_____

_____

_____

OUR CHURCH
MAKES A DIFFERENCE

Saint Philip Neri

A Cheerful Saint

Our belief in the Resurrection of Christ and our own hope of life forever give us the power to see the world in a new light. We celebrate that vision in many ways, one of which is seeing the good side of things. Saint Philip Neri (1515–1595) exemplified this trait. Philip's sense of humor and spirit of cheerfulness became well known.

Philip was born in Florence, Italy, and lived most of his life in Rome. At one point, while living in Rome, he became overcome at the disarray of the Church. He decided to get on with his life and move away from Rome and serve the Church as a missionary. This, however, was not in God's plan.

Philip became a priest in 1551. In 1564 he gathered many of his followers and fellow priests into an oratory, a place of prayer connected to a local church. He told the young men, "I will have no sadness in my house."

Philip's fondness for laughter and pranks earned him many critics, who thought of him as a fool and a clown. Nevertheless, the "fool" influenced many of the church leaders of his day. They delighted in his friendship and sought his advice.

Philip became known as the "Apostle of Rome." He was a messenger of hope and new life at a time when the Church really needed that vision. This holy clown of God founded forty-five oratories and a religious order, the Oratorians. Philip was canonized a saint in 1622.

How can you share the Gospel with hope and cheerfulness?

Members of the Oratorians

WHAT DIFFERENCE
Does Faith Make in My Life?

Renewed Effort and Perseverance

Jesus' Resurrection to new life and Ascension to his Father had a tremendous impact on his disciples. It renewed their faith and changed their lives forever. The Resurrection and Ascension gave them the perseverance to continue forward and spread the Good News. The Resurrection and Ascension have changed our lives forever too.

Your faith in the Risen and Glorified Christ supports you in the many transitions to new life you are called to make each day. There are times when you may feel defeated. What you need to remember is that God will give you the strength and courage to renew your commitment and try again. You can pick yourself up, change what needs to be changed, and continue on.

Here are four skills that may help you continue on.

1. **Use positive self-talk.** Self-talk is something we do all the time in the privacy of our own minds. Self-talk can either build you up or tear you down.

   Negative self-talk is the message that will make you feel that trying to do any better is not worth the effort. Negative self-talk stifles perseverance.

   Positive self-talk, such as "I can and will do better next time," is changing negative self-talk and affirming your efforts to do better. Positive self-talk strengthens perseverance.

2. Cancel or delete the negative messages of self-talk. One way to try to rid your head of negative messages is to say after the negative thought, "Cancel" or "Delete." After you cancel or delete the negative message, replace it immediately with a positive message. You may have to cancel the negative message many times as you practice this new skill. For example, you will need to practice this cancel or delete strategy every time you hear yourself or someone else put you down.

3. Accept constructive criticism. Respond positively to the advice of a friend, a parent, a coach, or a teacher when they ask you to evaluate your behavior. Constructive criticism is meant to help you, not to hurt you or put you down. Constructive criticism is a gift that can help you learn and grow in many ways, but only if you are open to responding positively to it.

4. Pray to the Holy Spirit. Ask the Holy Spirit to strengthen you with the gifts of courage, perseverance, and hope. Remember and trust that the Holy Spirit dwells within you. He is always with you to be your helper.

Faith Decision

- List some of the negative messages you send yourself. Turn each to a positive message and copy it on a sticky note. Post it in a place you will see it.

- Be consistent in practicing positive self-talk. Before you know it you will find yourself becoming your own best friend.

This week I will ask the Holy Spirit to help me change any negative self-talk to positive self-talk by

_____

_____

_____.

Christ, Our Hope

Reader 1:
Lord Jesus Christ,
you are the mediator
between God and us.

All: Christ, be our hope.

Reader 2:
You are judge of the world
and Lord of hosts.

All: Christ, be our hope.

Reader 3:
You ascended
not to distance yourself
from our lowly state.

All: Christ, be our hope.

Reader 4:
You ascended
that we might be confident
of following where you,
our Head and Founder,
have gone before.

All: Christ, be our hope.

BASED ON PREFACE I OF THE
ASCENSION OF THE LORD, ROMAN MISSAL

FAITH VOCABULARY

Define each of these faith terms:

1. Resurrection
2. Ascension
3. particular judgement
4. Last Judgment
5. heaven
6. purgatory
7. hell

MAIN IDEAS

Choose either (a) or (b) from each set of items. Write a brief paragraph to answer each of your choices.

1. (a) Compare the Resurrection of Christ as a historical event and as a mystery of faith.
   (b) Explain the significance of the Ascension for our lives.

2. (a) Explain why the death-Resurrection-Ascension of Jesus strengthens our hope.
   (b) Describe the Christian belief that at the end of time there will be a new heaven and earth.

CRITICAL THINKING

Using what you have learned in this chapter, briefly explain this statement:
At the moment of our death, life is changed, not ended.

FAMILY DISCUSSION

How is our family a living symbol of hope?

For more ideas on ways your family can live your faith, visit the "Faith First for Families" page at **www.FaithFirst.com**. Click on the Teen Center and read the saint of the week.

A Resurrection Story

A Scripture Story

FAITH FOCUS

What is the importance of the Risen Jesus appearing to the disciples?

FAITH VOCABULARY

Resurrection stories

What enjoyable breakfast memories do you have from your family?

Sometimes breakfast is a hurried meal, and sometimes it is skipped altogether. Yet a healthy breakfast gets us off to a good start.

It may come as a surprise that one of the Resurrection stories in the Gospels is a well-known breakfast story. The Risen Jesus appeared to his disciples early in the morning and invited the disciples to come eat breakfast with him.

What other times do you remember when the Risen Jesus appeared to his disciples?

Sea of Galilee coastline

Jesus said to them, "Come, have breakfast." And none of the disciples dared to ask him "Who are you?" because they realized it was the Lord.

JOHN 21:12

Testimonies to Jesus' Resurrection

There are many stories in the Gospels that tell us of Jesus appearing to his disciples after his Resurrection. Each of these **Resurrection stories** gives the testimony of the Church both to the fact of Jesus' Resurrection and her faith in it. Here is a list and a brief description of these stories:

- Matthew 28:8–17. The Risen Christ appears to the disciples and the women on a mountainside in Galilee.
- Mark 16:9–18. The Risen Christ appears first to Mary Magdalene; second, to two disciples walking; and third, to eleven disciples at table. All of these appearances take place in Jerusalem.
- Luke 24:1–49. The Risen Christ appears first to Peter. He next appears to two disciples walking on the road to Emmaus. Then he appears to the eleven disciples in Jerusalem.
- John 20:11–31. The Risen Christ first appears in Galilee to Mary of Magdala and then to the disciples, without Thomas. A week later he appears again to the disciples. This time Thomas is with them.
- John 21:1–23. The Risen Christ appears to seven disciples at the Sea of Tiberias.

Choose one of the Resurrection stories. Look it up and read it. Share with a partner what testimony it provides for Jesus' Resurrection.

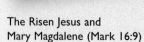

The Risen Jesus and Mary Magdalene (Mark 16:9)

The Risen Jesus and Saint Thomas (John 20:26–29)

"My Lord and My God"

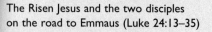

The Risen Jesus and the two disciples on the road to Emmaus (Luke 24:13–35)

Kidron Valley at the foot
of the Mount of Olives

The Resurrection Stories

Keeping the following four points in mind will help you understand the meaning of the Resurrection stories.

Pattern

There is a common pattern to each story. First, the disciple initially does not recognize Jesus. Second, Jesus does something, for example, he addresses a disciple by name. Third, the disciple comes to know that it is truly the Risen Lord.

Audience

Each account of the Gospel was first written to a particular audience, or community of the early Church. It was important that an eyewitness well known to each community tell the story of Jesus' Resurrection to that community.

Setting or location

The Jerusalem and the Galilean communities of the early Church told the Resurrection stories using places that would have local familiarity. This created greater interest, and the people would be better able to remember them.

Faith testimonies

The Gospel accounts of the appearances of the Risen Jesus to his disciples are testimonies to the event of the Resurrection itself. The variances in each story help make the story more understandable and memorable.

Each Resurrection story paints a vivid picture of the personal interaction between the Risen Christ and an individual disciple or group of disciples. Each time the disciples are assured that Jesus who had died and was buried had truly been raised from the dead.

View of Sea of Galilee from the Mount of Beatitudes

FAITH CONNECTION

How would you respond to a school friend who says he or she does not believe that the Resurrection really happened?

_____

_____

_____

Reading the Word of God

The Voice from the Shore

Peter and other disciples of Jesus were fishermen by trade. They came from Galilee and from families who made their living fishing on the Sea of Tiberias, which is also called the Sea of Galilee. It is no surprise then that after Jesus' death, we find them back home at work.

The Resurrection story in John 21:1–31 opens with Peter and the others doing what they had always done before they first met Jesus—fishing by casting their nets into the waters. The sun was rising over the eastern shore of the Sea of Tiberias. Peter, Thomas, Nathanael, James, John, and two other disciples were finishing up their night's work of fishing on the lake. Their empty boat and nets were all they had to show for their efforts. Suddenly, the silence over the lake was broken.

John begins the account of the appearances of the Risen Christ to the disciples this way:

> Jesus said to them, "Children, have you caught anything to eat?" They answered him, "No." So he said to them, "Cast the net over the right side of the boat and you will find something." So they cast it, and were not able to pull it in because of the number of fish. So the disciple whom Jesus loved said to Peter, "It is the Lord."

Christ Appears on the Borders of the Tiberius Sea. James J. Tissot

Second Miraculous Draught of Fishes. James J. Tissot

When Simon Peter heard that it was the Lord, he tucked in his garment, for he was lightly clad, and jumped into the sea. The other disciples came in the boat, for they were not far from shore, only about a hundred yards, dragging the net with the fish. When they climbed out on shore, they saw a charcoal fire with fish on it and bread. Jesus said to them, "Bring some of the fish you just caught." So Simon Peter went over and dragged the net ashore full of one hundred fifty-three large fish. Even though there were so many, the net was not torn. Jesus said to them, "Come, have breakfast." And none of the disciples dared to ask him, "Who are you?" because they realized it was the Lord. Jesus came over and took the bread and gave it to them, and in like manner the fish. This was now the third time Jesus was revealed to his disciples after being raised from the dead.   JOHN 21:5–14

Jesus also calls us. He calls us to be fishers of men and women. We are to bring others to know and recognize that Jesus was raised from the dead and lives. Jesus is the Lord.

Describe what happened when the disciples recognized the Risen Lord on the shore.

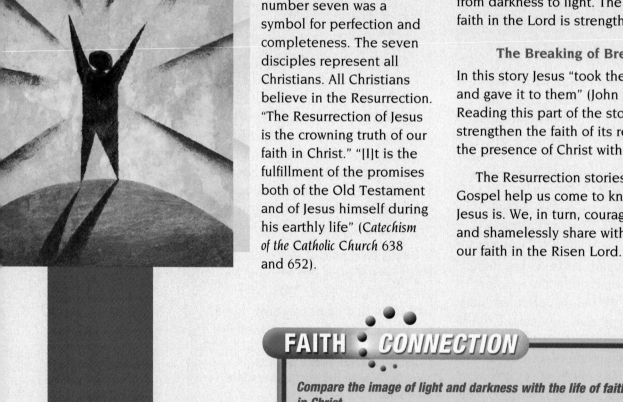

Symbols in the Story

John the Evangelist, as he does often in his account of the Gospel, uses signs or symbols in John 21:1–14. Identifying these symbols and their meanings helps us see and understand the faith meaning of the story.

The Number Seven

In this Resurrection story the Risen Jesus appears to "seven" disciples. Why seven and not eleven? For the original audience for whom John's account of the Gospel was written, the number seven was a symbol for perfection and completeness. The seven disciples represent all Christians. All Christians believe in the Resurrection. "The Resurrection of Jesus is the crowning truth of our faith in Christ." "[I]t is the fulfillment of the promises both of the Old Testament and of Jesus himself during his earthly life" (*Catechism of the Catholic Church* 638 and 652).

Light and Darkness

Part of the setting of the story is the movement of the disciples from darkness (fishing all night) to light (dawn). During the night they have no success. At dawn the Risen Christ, the Light of the world, orders the disciples to cast their nets into the water once again. Their fishing is successful beyond their wildest expectations. At the moment of their success the disciples recognize that the man who had called out to them is "the Lord" (John 21:7). The disciples see (believe) and go to the shore to meet the Risen Jesus. They move from darkness to light. The disciples' faith in the Lord is strengthened.

The Breaking of Bread

In this story Jesus "took the bread and gave it to them" (John 21:13). Reading this part of the story would strengthen the faith of its readers in the presence of Christ with them.

The Resurrection stories in the Gospel help us come to know who Jesus is. We, in turn, courageously and shamelessly share with others our faith in the Risen Lord.

FAITH CONNECTION

Compare the image of light and darkness with the life of faith in Christ.

_____

_____

_____

OUR CHURCH
MAKES A DIFFERENCE

Stained-Glass Windows

Christian artists proclaim and share their faith in Jesus in many creative, inspiring ways, including the design and creation of stained-glass windows. As early as the fourth century, Christians were making stained-glass windows. The best examples of stained glass were made in Europe, especially in France, during the twelfth and thirteenth centuries. Stained glass became important in churches during the Middle Ages (ca. A.D. 500–1500) for two main reasons.

First, stained-glass windows were a source of brilliant light. Since there was no electricity, churches depended upon natural light. The bubbles, flaws, and irregularities of stained-glass windows diffuse the light and make the glass sparkle.

Second, stained-glass windows were well-suited for sharing the faith. The symbolism of light and darkness permeates our faith.

The complex truths of good and evil, knowledge and ignorance can better be understood through pictures and symbols illuminated with color and light. For example, in the Middle Ages, when many people could not read, the pictures in the windows passed on the story of the faith of the Church from generation to generation. In the cathedral of Chartres, France, the entire Bible story, from Genesis to Revelation, is depicted in the rich glass hues of reds and blues.

The brilliance of the colors intertwining and reflecting off floors and walls surrounded people of faith with the presence of God. Imagine how easily believers could put themselves in the pictures and become part of the many stories that were unfolded before their eyes.

How can you share your faith in the Risen Jesus in a way that would capture the attention of people today?

The Life of Christ, stained-glass window, Notre Dame Cathedral, Chartres, France

WHAT DIFFERENCE

Does Faith Make in My Life?

Faith Sharing

The Resurrection stories are a testimony of faith that Jesus was raised from the dead and seen by his disciples. As you know, the disciples were so filled with faith that they began to share it with others.

As disciples of Jesus today, we too are called to share our faith in Jesus with others. Just as the early Church did, we too have good news to tell! Jesus was raised from the dead. He is Lord and Savior.

Here are a few suggestions of ways you can grow in your understanding of the faith of the Catholic Church and share that faith with others.

† Have a discussion with a friend or family member about what your faith means to you.
† Make a habit of reading the Bible at least once a week and sharing what you have read with someone else.
† Take part regularly in the celebration of Mass.

- † Volunteer to work on a parish project or committee that reaches out to help those in need.
- † Participate in your religion classes by sharing your thoughts, questions, and concerns.
- † Help organize and participate in a prayer service, retreat day, or the celebration of Mass in your parish or school.
- † Volunteer to be a reader at Mass.
- † Help a younger brother or sister learn their prayers or read them a Bible story.
- † Be willing to stand up for what is right even when it means going against the crowd.

Faith Decision

- In a small group talk about why you find it easy or difficult to share your faith with others.
- Brainstorm a list of ways of overcoming obstacles to sharing your faith. Role-play overcoming one of the obstacles on your list for your class.

This week I will share my faith with others by

_____

_____

_____

The Lord Is Risen

Leader:
At the Sea of Tiberias, Jesus
showed himself to the disciples.
All:
Jesus, you are Lord!

Leader:
The disciples' nets were empty.
All:
Jesus, you are Lord!

Leader:
Jesus had the disciples
cast their nets another way,
and their nets were filled
    to overflowing.
All:
Jesus, you are Lord!

Leader:
Then Peter recognized Jesus
    on the shore
and jumped into the water.
All:
Jesus, you are Lord!

Leader:
The disciples brought the fish
that they had caught
and dined together
at the break of day.
All:
Jesus, you are Lord!

Leader:
Jesus took bread and
    gave it to them.
He did the same with the fish.
All:
Jesus, you are Lord!

BASED ON JOHN 21:1–14

FAITH VOCABULARY

Define the faith term:

Resurrection stories

MAIN IDEAS

Choose either (a) or (b) from each set of items.
Write a brief paragraph to answer each of
your choices.

1. (a) Explain the importance of the Risen
       Jesus appearing to his disciples.
   (b) Outline and summarize the structure
       of the Resurrection stories in the
       Gospel.
2. (a) Describe what happened when the
       Risen Jesus called out to his disciples
       from the shore of the Sea of Tiberias.
   (b) Explain the use of the image of the
       number seven, light and darkness, or
       the breaking of bread in John 21:1–14.

CRITICAL THINKING

Using what you have learned in this chapter,
compare the words *seeing* and *believing*.

FAMILY DISCUSSION

How do we as a family share our faith in the
Risen Jesus with one another?

For more ideas on ways
your family can live your
faith, visit the "Faith First
for Families" page at
www.FaithFirst.com. Check
out the most recent games
on the Teen Center.

The Holy Spirit, the Sanctifier

The seven Gifts of the Holy Spirit

FAITH FOCUS

Why is the Holy Spirit vital to the Church?

FAITH VOCABULARY

Holy Spirit

Advocate

Annunciation

charisms

What experiences of wind have you had?

Cool breezes refresh and renew us on hot summer days. Violent gales frighten us as twisters bear down on our communities or hurricanes approach our coastlines. Children lie outdoors on their backs and watch clouds scuttle across the sky. Whether delightful or devastating, the power of air and wind has the ability to awe us.

The Hebrew word that means "breath" or "wind" is used for the word *spirit* in the Bible. From the wind hovering over the waters of creation in Genesis to the wind that filled the upper room in Jerusalem, the image of wind has been a sign that the Holy Spirit has been and is active at work in the world.

What does the image of wind help you understand about the work of the Holy Spirit?

And suddenly there came from the sky a noise like a strong driving wind. . . . Then there appeared to them tongues as of fire. . . . And they were all filled with the holy Spirit.

ACTS OF THE APOSTLES 2:2–4

123

The Holy Spirit: The Giver of Life

The Spirit of God

Throughout the Old Testament you will find few direct references to the **Holy Spirit.** But that does not mean that the Holy Spirit was not at work in the world bringing about God's plan of goodness. Often as invisible as breathing and breezes, the Holy Spirit was at work throughout the ages before the birth of Jesus. Whether in the burning bush or in a flash of lightning or the visit of mysterious strangers, the Holy Spirit was breathing energy into God's people.

*Ezekiel and
the Dry Bones*

The prophets spoke of a divine spirit who would be poured out into the hearts of all the people. This "spirit of the LORD" would be the source of new life for God's people. In the Book of the Prophet Ezekiel we read:

> The hand of the LORD came upon me, and he led me out in the spirit of the LORD and set me in the center of the plain, which was now filled with bones. He made me walk among them in every direction so that I saw how many they were on the surface of the plain. How dry they were! He asked me: Son of man, can these bones come to life? "Lord GOD," I answered, "you alone know that." . . . Then he said to me: Son of man, these bones are the whole house of Israel. . . . Therefore, prophesy and say to them: . . . I will put my spirit in you that you may live, and I will settle you upon your land; thus you shall know that I am the LORD. I have promised, and I will do it, says the LORD.
>
> EZEKIEL 37:1–3, 11, 12, 14

The Holy Spirit breathed life into the people of the Old Testament. However, it is only through Jesus Christ that the Holy Spirit's role in the divine plan becomes clear.

Describe the work of the Holy Spirit among God's people of the Old Covenant.

I will put my spirit in you that you may live.

Ezekiel 37:14

Did you Know...

Ezekiel the Prophet was sent to live in exile in Babylonia after the Babylonians destroyed the Temple in Jerusalem. It was there that Ezekiel brought God's word to the people. The name *Ezekiel* means "may God strengthen." Ezekiel's message strengthened the people with hope during the Babylonian Captivity (587–537 B.C.).

The Holy Spirit in the Gospel

The Gospel often presents Jesus and the Holy Spirit together. While distinct Persons of the Holy Trinity, the Son and the Holy Spirit are indeed inseparable. Their role in the divine plan of salvation is always connected. Whenever God the Father sends the Son, he always sends the Holy Spirit.

The Spirit and the Son

In the Gospel story of the **Annunciation** (a word meaning "announcement"), Jesus and the Holy Spirit are linked together. The angel Gabriel announced to Mary that God would implement his plan in her through the Holy Spirit (see Luke 1:35). With these words of the angel, the mission of the Holy Spirit begins to be revealed. The Holy Spirit prepared Mary to be the mother of the Redeemer, Jesus. Through Mary the Holy Spirit begins the great work of connecting the human family together in Jesus Christ, her only Son.

The Advocate and Helper

Jesus assured his disciples that his heavenly Father would "give the holy Spirit to those who ask him" (Luke 11:13). In the same vein, Jesus promised the Apostles that they would be put on trial. He told them that when the time came "[I]t will not be you who speak but the Spirit of your Father speaking through you" (Matthew 10:20). As Jesus' own trial approached, he pledged that the Holy Spirit, the **Advocate,** would come to the disciples (see John 14:26). An advocate is one who stands by a person's side, speaking and standing up for them.

Describe the connection between the work of the Holy Spirit and the work of Jesus.

FAITH CONNECTION

With a partner draw up a list of situations in which it is difficult to live your faith in Christ. Choose one and silently pray to the Holy Spirit to help you.

_____

_____

_____

125

The Holy Spirit in Our Lives

The Holy Spirit, the Advocate, is so close to us that we are temples of the Holy Spirit. He is like our breath, which is a vital element for our survival. Very often we do not even realize we are breathing because it is so much a part of our lives—so necessary for us to live. The Holy Spirit is like that.

Jesus tells his friend Nicodemus that "no one can enter the kingdom of God without being born of water and Spirit" (John 3:5). When Jesus discloses that his own body will be food for the world, Jesus describes the Holy Spirit, the giver of life (see John 6:63).

The Holy Spirit

- is given to us at Baptism and dwells within us.
- gives us the courage to live as disciples of Christ.
- teaches us to pray.
- is our teacher, reminding us of Christ and instructing us in everything.
- calls us to cooperate with him in using our gifts to build the Church.

Little by little, Jesus unveiled the reality and work, or mission, of the Holy Spirit. Eventually the Church would come to understand that the Holy Spirit is the third Person of the Holy Trinity.

Describe ways the Holy Spirit is present in your life.

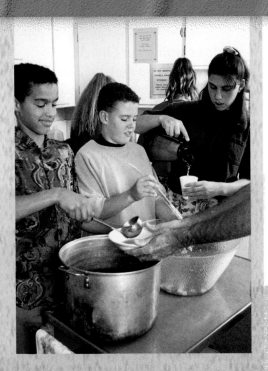

The Holy Spirit is the principal agent of the Church's mission. The Holy Spirit guides the pope and bishops in their ministry of serving the Church. Through the power of the Holy Spirit, Christ is present in the sacraments, especially in the Eucharist and in the word of God proclaimed in Scripture.

Christians have expressed their faith in the Holy Spirit in the Gospel story of John baptizing Jesus at the Jordan River. The image of a dove represents the Holy Spirit. The voice from heaven represents the Father. You can read this story in Matthew 3:13–17. The story is also told in Mark 1:9–11, Luke 3:21–22, and John 1:31–34.

Source of Unity

The Holy Spirit enables the Church to become one with God and empowers her to create a better world. By being members of the Church, we participate in the works of God being performed here and now, in and through the Church.

The Church Begins Her Mission

If you wondered how the Church has thrived for nearly two thousand years, look no further than the Holy Spirit. Just as Christ and the Church are inseparable, so also are the Church and the Holy Spirit. The Church's mission is the very mission of Christ and the Holy Spirit.

On the day of Pentecost, Jesus' mission on earth was fulfilled, and the work of the Holy Spirit, in a sense, took center stage. With the coming of the Holy Spirit, the Church was born. The Holy Spirit plays many roles in the Church.

Life Force of the Church

The Holy Spirit breathes life into each of us and into the Body of Christ, the Church. Christ, the Head of the Church, constantly pours out the Holy Spirit on the Church. The Holy Spirit nourishes the People of God, heals the Church, and helps the members of the Church act in harmony.

The Holy Spirit is the source of the Church's unity. He unites all of the Church's different parts into a unified whole, so that everything works together according to God's plan.

Describe the role of the Holy Spirit in the mission of the Church.

127

Temple of the Spirit

The Holy Spirit works in and through every member of the Church and is the source of her many **charisms**. Charisms are gifts or graces freely given to individual Christians for the benefit of building up the Church. The greatest of these charisms is the charism of love, or charity (see 1 Corinthians 13:13).

Out of the enormous diversity of the gifts and talents given to the Church, the Holy Spirit brings her a remarkable harmony and peace. The Holy Spirit ensures that Christ is the Head of the Body. The Holy Spirit lives within the Church, animating and directing the Church to continue bringing about God's plan of creation and salvation until the end of time.

Saint Augustine of Hippo said, "What the soul is to the human body, the Holy Spirit is to the Body of Christ, which is the Church." Augustine reworded what Saint Paul the Apostle said even more directly: "Do you not know that you are the temple of God, and that the Spirit of God dwells in you?"(1 Corinthians 3:16). "[W]e are the temple of the living God" (2 Corinthians 6:16). Without the Holy Spirit, the Church would not exist.

The Church's mission is to announce, bear witness to, and make present the life of the Trinity. To help the Church fulfill this role in the world, the Holy Spirit constantly builds up, inspires, animates, and blesses the Church until Christ comes again in glory at the end of time.

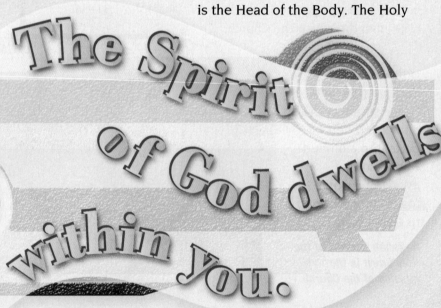

The Spirit of God dwells within you.

FAITH CONNECTION

What gifts, or charisms, have you received from the Holy Spirit? How are you using these charisms to take part in the mission, or work, of the Church?

_____

_____

_____

_____

OUR CHURCH MAKES A DIFFERENCE

Christian Art

The Holy Spirit has blessed us with the gift of creativity. One of the many ways Christians have expressed this gift to build up the Body of Christ is through art.

From the days of the early Church, Christians have shared their faith with others through the visual arts. Early Christian art used statues and mosaics to depict images of Christ and the miracles that demonstrated the saving power of God. In the seventh and eighth centuries, Irish missionaries needed liturgical books. Artistic centers arose where monks copied books and lavishly illustrated them with gold and other brilliant colors.

During the Renaissance (c. 1300–1600) the popes commissioned artists to work for the Church. In 1503 Pope Julius II began the rebuilding of Saint Peter's Basilica. He commissioned Michelangelo (1475–1564) to paint the ceiling of the Sistine Chapel and to create other major sculptures and monuments. Painters such as El Greco (1541–1614) captured the spiritual fervor of the Church. Architects and stone masons and sculptors used their gifts to raise magnificent cathedrals in praise of the grandeur of God. All these masterpieces of faith continue to be admired by both Christians and non-Christians.

Pope John Paul II, in a letter to artists dated April 4, 1999, invited artists to rediscover the depth of the spiritual and religious dimension that has been typical of art in its noblest forms in every age. Future Christian artists will continue to use the Holy Spirit's gift of creativity to celebrate and share their faith in God until Christ comes in glory at the end of time.

What forms of Christian art help you deepen your faith in God?

Saint Francis of Assisi, paint on wood

The Annunciation to the Shepherds: Book of Hours (c. 1450–1475), decorated vellum leaf. Simon Marmion (c. 1425–1489), French artist.

WHAT
DIFFERENCE
Does Faith Make in My Life?

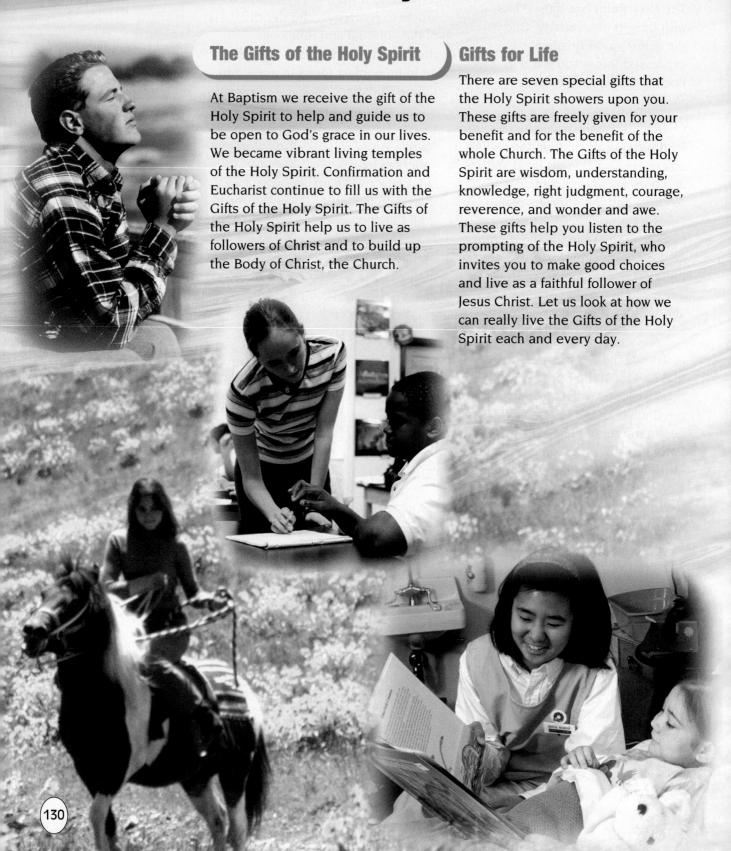

The Gifts of the Holy Spirit

At Baptism we receive the gift of the Holy Spirit to help and guide us to be open to God's grace in our lives. We became vibrant living temples of the Holy Spirit. Confirmation and Eucharist continue to fill us with the Gifts of the Holy Spirit. The Gifts of the Holy Spirit help us to live as followers of Christ and to build up the Body of Christ, the Church.

Gifts for Life

There are seven special gifts that the Holy Spirit showers upon you. These gifts are freely given for your benefit and for the benefit of the whole Church. The Gifts of the Holy Spirit are wisdom, understanding, knowledge, right judgment, courage, reverence, and wonder and awe. These gifts help you listen to the prompting of the Holy Spirit, who invites you to make good choices and live as a faithful follower of Jesus Christ. Let us look at how we can really live the Gifts of the Holy Spirit each and every day.

❖ *Wisdom* is the gift of knowing the right choices to make to live a holy life. The gift of wisdom helps you avoid the things that could lead you away from God.

❖ *Understanding* is the gift of comprehension, or the ability to grasp the teachings of the Church. The gift of understanding helps you be tolerant and sympathetic of others. It helps you sense when someone is hurting or in need of compassion.

❖ *Knowledge* is the gift of knowing and enlightenment. The gift of knowledge enables you to choose the right path that will lead you to God. It encourages you to avoid obstacles that will keep you from him.

❖ *Right Judgment, or Counsel,* is the gift of prudence. The gift of right judgment helps you make choices to live as a faithful follower of Jesus.

❖ *Courage, or Fortitude,* is the gift that helps you stand up for your faith in Christ. The gift of courage helps you overcome any obstacles that would keep you from practicing your faith.

❖ *Reverence, or Piety,* is the gift of confidence in God. This gift of reverence inspires you to joyfully want to serve God and others.

❖ *Wonder and Awe, or Fear of the Lord* is the gift of wonder and respect that encourages you to be in awe of God. The gift of wonder and awe moves you to so love God that you do not want to offend him by your words or actions.

Faith · · Decision

Describe how using the Gifts of the Holy Spirit would make a positive change in the world. On the first line, write one of the Gifts of the Holy Spirit. On the second line, write the effect of using it.

_____

_____

This week I will use the gifts named above and ask the Holy Spirit to help me live as a faithful follower of Jesus by

_____

_____

_____.

Prayer to the Holy Spirit

Leader: Breathe into me,
Holy Spirit,

All: that all my thoughts
may be holy.

Leader: Move in me,
Holy Spirit,

All: that my work, too,
may be holy.

Leader: Attract my heart,
Holy Spirit,

All: that I may love only
what is holy.

Leader: Strengthen me,
Holy Spirit,

All: that I may defend all
that is holy.

Leader: Protect me,
Holy Spirit,

All: that I always may
be holy. Amen.

FAITH VOCABULARY

Define each of these faith terms:

1. Holy Spirit
2. Annunciation
3. Advocate
4. charisms

MAIN IDEAS

Choose either (a) or (b) from each set of items. Write a brief paragraph to answer each of your choices.

1. (a) Describe the work of the Holy Spirit among the People of God in the Old Testament.
   (b) Discuss the relationship between the work of Jesus and the work of the Holy Spirit.

2. (a) Explain how the Holy Spirit is our advocate.
   (b) Discuss the work of the Holy Spirit and the mission of the Church.

CRITICAL THINKING

Using what you have learned in this chapter, briefly explain what you profess in the Nicene Creed when you say:
"We believe in the Holy Spirit, the Lord, the giver of life."

FAMILY DISCUSSION

How can we cooperate with the Holy Spirit and work toward building a deeper unity and harmony within our family?

For more ideas on ways your family can live your faith, visit the "Faith First for Families" page at **www.FaithFirst.com**. Go to the Teen Center to find additional activities for this chapter.

UNIT TWO
REVIEWREVIEW

A. The Best Answer

Read each statement and circle the best answer.

1. What word does the New Testament use for Jesus that is a profession of the Church's faith in his divinity?
   A. Christ
   B. Messiah
   C. Lord
   D. Savior

2. What term does the Church use to name the dogma of the Son of God becoming man?
   A. Incarnation
   B. Annunciation
   C. Immaculate Conception
   D. Crucifixion

3. What term does the Church use to describe Christ's action of delivering us from sin and death?
   A. Incarnation
   B. Ascension
   C. Immaculate Conception
   D. expiation

4. What term does the Church use to name the return of the Risen Jesus to his Father in heaven?
   A. Ascension
   B. Annunciation
   C. Resurrection
   D. Pentecost

5. Which of these biblical titles describes the work of the Holy Spirit in the Church?
   A. Savior
   B. Lord
   C. Advocate
   D. Christ

B. Matching Words and Phrases

Match the terms in column A with the descriptions in column B.

Column A

____ 1. Immaculate Conception

____ 2. suffering Servant

____ 3. Messiah

____ 4. advocate

____ 5. original sin

____ 6. Transfiguration

____ 7. prophet

____ 8. Resurrection stories

____ 9. Last Judgment

____ 10. particular judgment

Column B

a. clarified the identity of Jesus and his ministry on earth

b. Hebrew term meaning "Anointed One"

c. Mary's preservation from sin from the first moment of her existence

d. the choice of evil over good by Adam and Eve that resulted in the weakening of human nature

e. image of the Jesus described by Isaiah the Prophet

f. the assignment of our souls to heaven, purgatory, or hell at the moment of our death

g. the appearance of all souls in their resurrected bodies when Christ will show his identity

h. the accounts in the Gospels of the Risen Lord's appearances to his disciples

i. someone who stands by a person's side, speaking and standing up for them

j. Greek word meaning "one who speaks before others"

C. What I Have Learned

Using what you learned in Unit Two, write a two-sentence reflection about each of these statements.

1. We believe and hope that God will never abandon us.

_____

_____

2. The Holy Spirit works in every member of the Church.

_____

_____

D. From a Scripture Story

On a separate sheet of paper do the following:

Describe how the suffering Servant in the Book of Isaiah helps you understand the Passion and death of Jesus. Tell how your experiences of suffering can help others endure their suffering.

Catholic Prayers and Practices

Sign of the Cross

In the name of the Father,
and of the Son,
and of the Holy Spirit. Amen.

Glory Be

Glory be to the Father
and to the Son
and to the Holy Spirit,
as it was in the beginning is now,
and ever shall be
world without end. Amen.

Lord's Prayer

Our Father, who art in heaven,
hallowed be thy name;
thy kingdom come,
thy will be done on earth
    as it is in heaven.
Give us this day our daily bread,
and forgive us our trespasses,
as we forgive those who trespass
    against us;
and lead us not into temptation,
but deliver us from evil. Amen.

Hail Mary

Hail, Mary, full of grace,
the Lord is with thee.
Blessed art thou among women,
and blessed is the fruit
    of thy womb, Jesus.
Holy Mary, Mother of God,
pray for us sinners,
now and at the hour of our death.
Amen.

Signum Crucis

In nómine Patris,
et Fílii,
et Spíritus Sancti. Amen.

Gloria Patri

Glória Patri
et Fílio
et Spirítui Sancto.
Sicut erat in princípio,
et nunc et semper
et in sæcula sæculórum. Amen.

Pater Noster

Pater noster, qui es in cælis:
sanctificétur nomen tuum;
advéniat regnum tuum;
fiat volúntas tua, sicut in cælo, et in terra.
Panem nostrum cotidiánum
    da nobis hódie;
et dimítte nobis débita nostra,
sicut et nos dimíttimus debitóribus nostris;
et ne nos indúcas in tentatiónem;
sed líbera nos a malo. Amen.

Ave, Maria

Ave, María, grátia plena,
Dóminus tecum.
Benedícta tu in muliéribus,
et benedíctus fructus ventris tui, Jesus.
Sancta María, Mater Dei,
ora pro nobis peccatóribus,
nunc et in hora mortis nostræ. Amen.

Nicene Creed

I believe in one God,
the Father almighty,
maker of heaven and earth,
of all things visible and invisible.

I believe in one Lord Jesus Christ,
the Only Begotten Son of God,
born of the Father before all ages.
God from God, Light from Light,
true God from true God,
begotten, not made, consubstantial
   with the Father;
through him all things were made.
For us men and for our salvation
he came down from heaven,
and by the Holy Spirit was incarnate
   of the Virgin Mary,
and became man.

For our sake he was crucified under
   Pontius Pilate,
he suffered death and was buried,
and rose again on the third day
in accordance with the Scriptures.
He ascended into heaven
and is seated at the right hand of the Father.
He will come again in glory
to judge the living and the dead
and his kingdom will have no end.

I believe in the Holy Spirit, the Lord,
   the giver of life,
who proceeds from the Father and the Son,
who with the Father and the Son
   is adored and glorified,
who has spoken through the prophets.

I believe in one, holy, catholic and
   apostolic Church.
I confess one Baptism for the forgiveness of sins
and I look forward to the resurrection of the dead
   and the life of the world to come.
Amen.

Apostles' Creed

I believe in God,
the Father almighty,
Creator of heaven and earth,
and in Jesus Christ, his only Son, our Lord,
who was conceived by the Holy Spirit,
born of the Virgin Mary,
suffered under Pontius Pilate,
was crucified, died and was buried;
he descended into hell;
on the third day he rose again from the dead;
he ascended into heaven,
and is seated at the right hand of God
   the Father almighty;
from there he will come to judge the living
   and the dead.

I believe in the Holy Spirit,
the holy catholic Church,
the communion of saints,
the forgiveness of sins,
the resurrection of the body,
and life everlasting. Amen.

Morning Prayer

Dear God,
as I begin this day,
keep me in your love and care.
Help me to live as your child today.
Bless me, my family, and my friends in all we do.
Keep us all close to you. Amen.

Evening Prayer

Dear God,
I thank you for today.
Keep me safe throughout the night.
Thank you for all the good I did today.
I am sorry for what I have chosen to do wrong.
Bless my family and friends. Amen.

Grace before Meals

Bless us, O Lord,
    and these thy gifts,
which we are about to receive
    from thy bounty,
through Christ our Lord. Amen.

Grace after Meals

We give thee thanks, for all thy benefits,
    almighty God,
who lives and reigns forever. Amen.

The Divine Praises

Blessed be God.
Blessed be his holy name.
Blessed be Jesus Christ, true God and true man.
Blessed be the name of Jesus.
Blessed be his most Sacred Heart.
Blessed be his most precious Blood.
Blessed be Jesus in the most holy Sacrament
    of the altar.
Blessed be the Holy Spirit, the Paraclete.
Blessed be the great Mother of God, Mary
    most holy.
Blessed be her holy and Immaculate
    Conception.
Blessed be her glorious Assumption.
Blessed be the name of Mary, Virgin and Mother.
Blessed be Saint Joseph, her most chaste spouse.
Blessed be God in his angels and in his saints.

Prayer to the Holy Spirit

Come, Holy Spirit, fill the hearts
    of your faithful.
And kindle in them the
    fire of your love.
Send forth your Spirit and
    they shall be created.
And you will renew the
    face of the earth.

Act of Faith

My God, I firmly believe that you are one God in three divine Persons, Father, Son, and Holy Spirit; I believe that your divine Son became man and died for our sins, and that he will come to judge the living and the dead. Amen.

Act of Hope

My God, relying on your infinite goodness and promises, I hope to obtain pardon of my sins, the help of your grace, and life everlasting, through the merits of Jesus Christ, my Lord and Redeemer. Amen.

Act of Love

My God, I love you above all things, with my whole heart and soul, because you are all good and worthy of all my love. I love my neighbor as myself for the love of you. I forgive all who have injured me and I ask pardon of all whom I have injured. Amen.

The Trinity,
stained glass

Magnificat

My soul proclaims the greatness
  of the Lord,
my spirit rejoices in God my Savior
for he has looked with favor
  on his lowly servant.

From this day all generations
  will call me blessed:
the Almighty has done great things
  for me,
and holy is his name.

He has mercy on those
  who fear him
in every generation.

He has shown the strength
  of his arm,
he has scattered the proud
  in their conceit.

He has cast down the mighty
  from their thrones,
and has lifted up the lowly.

He has filled the hungry
  with good things,
and the rich he has sent away empty.

He has come to the help
  of his servant Israel
for he has remembered
  his promise of mercy,
the promise he made to our fathers,
to Abraham and his children for ever.

BASED ON LUKE 1:46–55
FROM CATHOLIC HOUSEHOLD BLESSINGS AND PRAYERS

Memorare

Remember, O most gracious Virgin Mary,
that never was it known
that anyone who fled to your protection,
implored your help,
or sought your intercession was left unaided.

Inspired by this confidence,
I fly unto you, O Virgin of virgins, my mother;
to you do I come,
before you I stand, sinful and sorrowful.

O Mother of the Word Incarnate,
despise not my petitions,
but in your mercy
  hear and answer me.
Amen.

Our Lady
of the
Rosary

Rosary

Catholics pray the Rosary to honor Mary and remember the important events in the life of Jesus and Mary. We begin praying the Rosary by praying the Apostles' Creed, the Lord's Prayer, and three Hail Marys. Each mystery of the Rosary is prayed by praying the Lord's Prayer once, the Hail Mary ten times, and the Glory Be once. When we have finished the last mystery, we pray the Hail, Holy Queen.

Joyful Mysteries

1. The Annunciation
2. The Visitation
3. The Nativity
4. The Presentation in the Temple
5. The Finding of the Child Jesus
   After Three Days in the Temple

Luminous Mysteries

1. The Baptism at the Jordan
2. The Miracle at Cana
3. The Proclamation of the Kingdom
   and the Call to Conversion
4. The Transfiguration
5. The Institution of the Eucharist

Sorrowful Mysteries

1. The Agony in the Garden
2. The Scourging at the Pillar
3. The Crowning with Thorns
4. The Carrying of the Cross
5. The Crucifixion and Death

Glorious Mysteries

1. The Resurrection
2. The Ascension
3. The Descent of the Holy Spirit at Pentecost
4. The Assumption of Mary
5. The Crowning of the Blessed Virgin
   as Queen of Heaven and Earth

Hail, Holy Queen

Hail, holy Queen, Mother of mercy:
Hail, our life, our sweetness
    and our hope.
To you do we cry, poor banished children of Eve.
To you do we send up our sighs,
mourning and weeping
    in this valley of tears.
Turn then, most gracious advocate,
your eyes of mercy toward us;
and after this our exile
show unto us the blessed fruit
    of your womb, Jesus.
O clement, O loving, O sweet
    Virgin Mary.

Stations of the Cross

1. Jesus is condemned to death.

2. Jesus accepts his cross.

3. Jesus falls the first time.

4. Jesus meets his mother.

5. Simon helps Jesus carry the cross.

6. Veronica wipes the face of Jesus.

7. Jesus falls the second time.

8. Jesus meets the women.

9. Jesus falls the third time.

10. Jesus is stripped of his clothes.

11. Jesus is nailed to the cross.

12. Jesus dies on the cross.

13. Jesus is taken down from the cross.

14. Jesus is buried in the tomb.

Some parishes conclude the Stations by reflecting on the Resurrection of Jesus.

The Great Commandment

"You shall love the Lord,
your God, with all your
heart, with all your soul,
and with all your mind. . . .
You shall love your neighbor as yourself."

MATTHEW 22:37, 39

The Ten Commandments

1. I am the LORD your God: you shall not have strange gods before me.
2. You shall not take the name of the LORD your God in vain.
3. Remember to keep holy the LORD's Day.
4. Honor your father and your mother.
5. You shall not kill.
6. You shall not commit adultery.
7. You shall not steal.
8. You shall not bear false witness against your neighbor.
9. You shall not covet your neighbor's wife.
10. You shall not covet your neighbor's goods.

Precepts of the Church

1. Participate in Mass on Sundays and holy days of obligation and rest from unnecessary work.
2. Confess sins at least once a year.
3. Receive Holy Communion at least during the Easter season.
4. Observe the prescribed days of fasting and abstinence.
5. Provide for the material needs of the Church, according to one's abilities.

The Beatitudes

"Blessed are the poor in spirit,
    for theirs is the kingdom of heaven.
Blessed are they who mourn,
    for they will be comforted.
Blessed are the meek,
    for they will inherit the land.
Blessed are they who hunger
        and thirst for righteousness,
    for they will be satisfied.
Blessed are the merciful,
    for they will be shown mercy.
Blessed are the clean of heart,
    for they will see God.
Blessed are the peacemakers,
    for they will be called children of God.
Blessed are they who are persecuted for the
        sake of righteousness,
    for theirs is the kingdom of heaven.

"Blessed are you when they insult you and persecute you and utter every kind of evil against you [falsely] because of me. Rejoice and be glad, for your reward will be great in heaven."

MATTHEW 5:3–12

The Beatitude Window,
stained glass.
Jerry Sodorff, artist

141

Theological Virtues

Faith
Hope
Love

Cardinal, or Moral, Virtues

Prudence
Justice
Fortitude
Temperance

Corporal Works of Mercy

Feed people who are hungry.
Give drink to people who are thirsty.
Clothe people who need clothes.
Visit prisoners.
Shelter people who are homeless.
Visit people who are sick.
Bury people who have died.

Spiritual Works of Mercy

Help people who sin.
Teach people who are ignorant.
Give advice to people who have doubts.
Comfort people who suffer.
Be patient with other people.
Forgive people who hurt you.
Pray for people who are alive and
    for those who have died.

Gifts of the Holy Spirit

Wisdom
Understanding
Right judgment (Counsel)
Courage (Fortitude)
Knowledge
Reverence (Piety)
Wonder and awe (Fear of the Lord)

Fruits of the Holy Spirit

love
joy
peace
patience
kindness
goodness
generosity
gentleness
faithfulness
modesty
self-control
chastity

Faith, Hope, and Charity, stained glass

Basic Principles of the Church's Teaching on Social Justice

The Church's teaching on social justice guides us in living lives of holiness and building a just society. These principles are:

1. All human life is sacred. The basic equality of all people flows from their dignity as human persons and the rights that flow from that dignity.

2. The human person is the principle, the object, and the subject of every social group.

3. The human person has been created by God to belong to and to participate in a family and other social communities.

4. Respect for the rights of people flows from their dignity as persons. Society and all social organizations must promote virtue and protect human life and human rights and guarantee the conditions that promote the exercise of freedom.

5. Political communities and public authority are based on human nature. They belong to an order established by God.

6. All human authority must be used for the common good of society.

7. The common good of society consists of respect for and promotion of the fundamental rights of the human person; the just development of material and spiritual goods of society; and the peace and safety of all people.

8. We need to work to eliminate the sinful inequalities that exist between peoples and for the improvement of the living conditions of people. The needs of the poor and vulnerable have a priority.

9. We are one human and global family. We are to share our spiritual blessings, even more than our material blessings.

Based on the *Catechism of the Catholic Church*

The Seven Sacraments

Jesus gave the Church the seven sacraments. The sacraments are the main liturgical signs of the Church. They make the Paschal Mystery of Jesus, who is always the main celebrant of each sacrament, present to us. They make us sharers in the saving work of Christ and in the life of the Holy Trinity.

Sacraments of Initiation

Baptism
We are joined to Jesus Christ, become members of the Church, receive the gift of the Holy Spirit, and are reborn as God's adopted children. Original and all personal sins are forgiven.

Confirmation
Our Baptism is sealed with the gift of the Holy Spirit.

Eucharist
We receive the Body and Blood of Christ who is truly and really present under the appearances of bread and wine. We share in the one sacrifice of Christ. Sharing in the Eucharist most fully joins us to Christ and to the Church.

Sacraments of Healing

Penance and Reconciliation
We receive God's gift of forgiveness and peace.

Anointing of the Sick
Jesus' work of healing is continued in our lives and strengthens our faith and trust in God when we are seriously ill or dying.

Sacraments at the Service of Communion

Holy Orders
A baptized man is ordained and consecrated to serve the Church as a bishop, priest, or deacon.

Matrimony
A baptized man and a baptized woman are united in a lifelong bond of faithful love. They become a sign of God's love for all people and of Christ's love for the Church.

Baptism   Eucharist   Confirmation   Matrimony

Penance and Reconciliation   Holy Orders   Anointing of the Sick

Celebrating the Mass

The Introductory Rites

The Entrance
Sign of the Cross
    and Greeting
The Penitential Act
The Gloria
The Collect

The Liturgy of the Word

The First Reading
    (Usually from the
    Old Testament)
The Psalm
The Second Reading
    (Usually from New
    Testament Letters)
The Gospel Acclamation
The Gospel
The Homily
The Profession of Faith
Prayer of the Faithful

The Liturgy of the Eucharist

The Preparation of the Gifts
The Prayer over the Offerings
The Eucharistic Prayer
The Communion Rite
    The Lord's Prayer
    The Sign of Peace
    The Fraction
    Communion
The Prayer After Communion

The Concluding Rites

The Greeting
The Blessing
The Dismissal

Celebrating Penance and Reconciliation

Individual Rite of Reconciliation

Greeting

Scripture Reading

Confession of Sins

Act of Contrition

Absolution

Closing Prayer

Communal Rite of Reconciliation

Greeting

Scripture Reading

Homily

Examination of Conscience with Litany of

    Contrition and the Lord's Prayer

Individual Confession and Absolution

Closing Prayer

Act of Contrition

My God,
I am sorry for my sins with all my heart.
In choosing to do wrong
and failing to do good,
I have sinned against you
whom I should love above all things.
I firmly intend, with your help,
to do penance,
to sin no more,
and to avoid whatever leads me to sin.
Our Savior Jesus Christ
suffered and died for us.
In his name, my God, have mercy.

The Books of the Bible

The Old Testament

Law (Torah) or Pentateuch

Genesis	(Gn)
Exodus	(Ex)
Leviticus	(Lv)
Numbers	(Nm)
Deuteronomy	(Dt)

Historical Books

Joshua	(Jos)
Judges	(Jgs)
Ruth	(Ru)
First Book of Samuel	(1 Sm)
Second Book of Samuel	(2 Sm)
First Book of Kings	(1 Kgs)
Second Book of Kings	(2 Kgs)
First Book of Chronicles	(1 Chr)
Second Book of Chronicles	(2 Chr)
Ezra	(Ezr)
Nehemiah	(Neh)
Tobit	(Tb)
Judith	(Jdt)
Esther	(Est)
First Book of Maccabees	(1 Mc)
Second Book of Maccabees	(2 Mc)

The Poetry and Wisdom Books

Job	(Jb)
Psalms	(Ps)
Proverbs	(Prv)
Ecclesiastes	(Eccl)
Song of Songs	(Sg)
Wisdom	(Wis)
Sirach/Ecclesiasticus	(Sir)

Prophets

Isaiah	(Is)
Jeremiah	(Jer)
Lamentations	(Lam)
Baruch	(Bar)
Ezekiel	(Ez)
Daniel	(Dn)
Hosea	(Hos)
Joel	(Jl)
Amos	(Am)
Obadiah	(Ob)
Jonah	(Jon)
Micah	(Mi)
Nahum	(Na)
Habakkuk	(Hb)
Zephaniah	(Zep)
Haggai	(Hg)
Zechariah	(Zec)
Malachi	(Mal)

The New Testament

The Gospels

Matthew	(Mt)
Mark	(Mk)
Luke	(Lk)
John	(Jn)

Early Church

Acts of the Apostles	(Acts)

Letters of Paul and Other Letters

Romans	(Rom)
First Letter to the Corinthians	(1 Cor)
Second Letter to the Corinthians	(2 Cor)
Galatians	(Gal)
Ephesians	(Eph)
Philippians	(Phil)
Colossians	(Col)
First Letter to the Thessalonians	(1 Thes)
Second Letter to the Thessalonians	(2 Thes)
First Letter to Timothy	(1 Tm)
Second Letter to Timothy	(2 Tm)
Titus	(Ti)
Philemon	(Phlm)
Hebrews	(Heb)
James	(Jas)
First Letter of Peter	(1 Pt)
Second Letter of Peter	(2 Pt)
First Letter of John	(1 Jn)
Second Letter of John	(2 Jn)
Third Letter of John	(3 Jn)
Jude	(Jude)

Revelation

Revelation	(Rv)

A

advocate

One who stands by a person's side, speaking for them, and standing up for them.

Advocate

The Holy Spirit, the third Person of the Holy Trinity.

Annunciation

The announcement by the angel Gabriel to Mary that she was chosen by God to become the Mother of Jesus, the Son of God, by the power of the Holy Spirit.

Ascension

The return of the Risen Christ in glory to his Father, to the world of the divine.

attribute

Qualities or characteristics that belong to a person or thing.

attributes of God

Qualities or characteristics that belong to God and that help us understand the mystery of God.

B

beatific vision

Seeing God face-to-face in heavenly glory.

Bible (Sacred Scripture)

The collection of all the writings God has inspired authors to write in his name.

blasphemy

The act of claiming to be God.

Body of Christ

An image for the Church used by Paul the Apostle that teaches that all the members of the Church are one in Christ, the Head of the Church, and that all members have a unique and important work in the Church.

Book of Signs

The first part of the Gospel according to John is called this because it includes many stories of miracles, or signs, in the life of Jesus.

C

canon of Sacred Scripture

The list of books that the Catholic Church has identified and teaches to be the inspired Word of God.

charisms

Gifts or graces freely given to individual Christians by the Holy Spirit for the benefit of building up the Church.

Church

The word *church* means "convocation, those called together." The Church is the sacrament of salvation—the sign and instrument of our reconciliation and communion with God and one another. The Body of Christ; the people God the Father has called together in Jesus Christ through the power of the Holy Spirit.

Communion of Saints

The communion, or unity, of all the redeemed, those living on earth, those being purified after death, and those enjoying life everlasting and eternal happiness with God, the angels, and Mary and all the saints.

Covenant

The solemn agreement of fidelity that God and the people of God freely entered into, which was renewed in Christ, the new and everlasting Covenant.

D

deposit of faith

The source of faith that is drawn from to pass on God's revelation to us; it is the unity of Scripture and Tradition.

divine missions

The particular works of God in each of the three Persons of the Holy Trinity. The work of creation is attributed to the Father, the work of salvation is attributed to the Son, and the work of sanctification, or our holiness, is attributed to the Holy Spirit.

divine nature

The heart of God's revelation of himself; that which makes God God.

divine Providence

God's caring love for us. The attribute of God that his almighty power and caring love is always with us.

divine Revelation

God making known the hidden mystery of who he is and the divine plan of creation and salvation known over time so that we can get to know him and love him better.

dogma of faith

A truth taught by the Church as revealed by God.

Glossary

eternal
Having no end; timeless; everlasting. The attribute that states that God always was and always will be.

Evangelist
Teller of the good news, or the Gospel. Matthew, Mark, Luke, and John, writers of the accounts of the Gospel in the New Testament.

everlasting
The attribute that states that God always was and always will be.

expiation
An act that takes away guilt or makes amends for a wrongdoing.

faith
The gift of God's invitation to us to believe and trust in him; it is also the power God gives us to respond to his invitation.

Fourth Gospel
Another name for the Gospel according to John.

heaven
Eternal life and happiness with God and the saints forever.

hell
The immediate and everlasting separation from God and the saints.

Holy Spirit
The third divine Person of the Holy Trinity sent to us by the Father in the name of his Son, Jesus.

Holy Trinity
The mystery of one God in three Persons—God the Father, God the Son, God the Holy Spirit.

Immaculate Conception
Mary was totally preserved from the stain of original sin from the very first moment of her existence, or conception, in her mother's womb. Mary did not commit any personal sin throughout her entire life.

Incarnation
A word meaning "take on flesh." It is the term the Church uses to name our belief that the Son of God truly became human while remaining truly God. Jesus is true God and true man.

inspiration of the Bible
The Holy Spirit guiding the human writers of Sacred Scripture so that they would faithfully and accurately communicate the word of God, who is the principal author of the Scriptures.

kingdom of God
The image used in the Bible to describe all people and creation living in communion with God. The kingdom will be fully realized when Christ comes again in glory at the end of time.

Last Judgment
The judgment at which all the humans will appear in their own bodies, give an account of their deeds, and Christ will show his identity with the least of his brothers and sisters.

literary genres
Styles of writing.

Lord
A title expressing our belief that Jesus is truly divine, or God. The word means "master, ruler, a person of authority." It is used in the Old Testament to name God.

Lord's Prayer
The Our Father; the prayer Jesus taught us to pray.

Magisterium
The teaching authority of the Church.

Messiah
A Hebrew term meaning "anointed one"; the Anointed One God promised to send his people. Jesus, the Messiah promised by God.

miracle
A wonderful sign of God working among people, inviting us to believe and trust in him. The word means "wonder, something marvelous." Jesus performed miracles to reveal God's love for people.

moral evil
The harm we willingly inflict on one another and on God's good creation.

mystery
The word we use to describe the fact that we can never fully comprehend or fully grasp God. God is, and his loving plan for us is, a mystery. We only know who God is and what his plan for us is because he has revealed it.

omnipresence
The attribute of God that he is always present to all of his creation.

oral tradition
The passing on of God's revelation by word of mouth.

original sin

Adam and Eve's choice of evil over obedience to God. The sin Adam and Eve committed by turning away from God by freely choosing to do what they knew God did not want them to do.

P-Q

particular judgment

The assignment given to our souls at death to their final destiny by Jesus based on what we have done in our lives.

Paschal Mystery

The saving events of the Passion, death, Resurrection, and glorious Ascension of Jesus Christ; the passing over of Jesus from death into a new and glorious life; the name we give to God's plan of saving us in Jesus Christ.

philosophers

People who use logical reasoning to study and discover truths about nature, life, morals, and God.

physical death

The separation of our immortal soul from our mortal body.

prophets

A Greek word meaning "those who speak before others"; those people whom God has chosen to speak in his name.

purgatory

An opportunity after death to purify and strengthen our love for God before we enter heaven.

R

redemption

Christ delivering us from sin and death through his Paschal Mystery.

Resurrection

Jesus being raised from the dead to a new glorified life.

Resurrection stories

Accounts in the Gospel that give testimony of the Church to the fact of Jesus' resurrection and her faith in it.

revelation

God's free gift of making himself known to us and giving himself to us by gradually communicating his own mystery in deeds and words.

S

Sacred Scripture (the Bible)

The collection of all the writings God has inspired authors to write in his name that are collected in the Bible.

Sacred Tradition

The passing on of our faith in Christ by the Church through the power and guidance of the Holy Spirit.

salvation

Humanity's deliverance from the power of sin and death through Jesus Christ who died for our sins in accordance with the Scriptures.

Satan

The serpent-tempter that enticed the first humans to test the limits of their freedom.

soul

The spiritual part of who we are that is immortal, or never dies. Our innermost being; that which bears the imprint of the image of God.

suffering Servant

An idealization, or perfect image, of the faithful Jew suffering in exile. This was to help the world acknowledge Yahweh as the one true God once the Jewish people were freed from exile. We believe that Jesus Christ is the suffering Servant described in the Book of the Prophet Isaiah.

T-X

temple of the Holy Spirit

The image used to describe the indwelling of the Spirit in the Church and within the hearts of the faithful.

theologians

People who study and deepen their understanding of the truths known by faith.

transfiguration

The word *transfiguration* means "a marked change in appearance, especially a change that glorifies."

Transfiguration

The mysterious change in appearance of Jesus in the presence of Peter, James, and John during which Jesus speaks with Moses and the Prophet Elijah; the manifestation of the divinity of Jesus Christ.

Y-Z

YHWH

The Hebrew letters for the name God revealed to Moses.

Index

A

Abraham, 23
Act of Contrition, 145
Act of Faith, 137
Act of Hope, 137
Act of Love, 137
Adam and Eve, 22, 44, 94–95
Advocate, 125
agnosticism, 13
alcohol, abuse of, 36
Amos, prophet, 23, 84
Annunciation, 125
Anointing of the Sick, sacrament of, 144
Apostles' Creed, 136
art, Christian, as expressions of faith, 129
Ascension, 74, 103, 105–106, 108
atheism, 13

B

Babylonian Captivity, 125
Baptism, sacrament of, 144
Beatitudes, 141
Benedictus, 72
Bible, 19–27
  Books of the, list of, 146
  as God's own word, 17, 20, 26
  Gospel as center, 21
  Holy Spirit and, 20
  inspiration of, 20, 26
  literary genre in, 21
  praying the, 25, 28
  Sacred Tradition and, 24
bishops, ministry of, 24
Book of Signs, 31
breaking of bread, 118

C

Camara, Archbishop Helder, 89
Canon of Sacred Scripture, 20, 146
cardinal virtues, 142
charisms, 128
Church
  and Holy Spirit,127–128
  mission of, 127–128
  as people of faith, 12
  as People of God, 127
  as teacher, 15, 24, 42
  as Temple of Holy Spirit, 128
Confirmation, sacrament of, 144
Constantine, Emperor, 51
Corporal Works of Mercy, 142
courage, gift of, 130–131
Covenant, 22–23
creation, 39–48
  Adam and Eve to care for, 94
  as revelation of God, 11–12, 17, 39–40
  as work of Trinity, 54
cross, veneration of, 88
Crucifixion, 95–97

D

David, King, 23
death, 107

disciples of Jesus, 87
  appearances to, by Risen Jesus, 114–118
  at Transfiguration, 76–77
divine missions of Holy Trinity, 53
Divine Praises, 137
divine Revelation, 13
dogma of faith, 52
domestic church, 55
drug abuse, 36

E

ecumenical council, 51–52, 66–67
Elijah the prophet, 74–78
Emmaus, 114
eternal life, 34, 91, 106–108
Eucharist, sacrament of
  celebration of, 105, 145
  rites of, 145
evangelists, 29
Evening Prayer, 137
evil, 94–95
Exodus, 74
expiation for sin, 96
Ezekiel, 23, 125

F

faith
  family as community of, 55
  as gift of God, 13
  in Jesus, 34, 51, 65
  and reason, 12
  and Sacred Tradition, 24
  and understanding, 14
faith, skills for living:
  balancing relationships, 56–57
  building relationships, 46–47
  communication skills, 26–27
  dealing with loss, 90–91
  faith sharing, 120–121
  getting in touch with God, 16–17
  gifts of the Holy Spirit, 130–131
  overcoming obstacles to seeing with eyes of faith, 36–37
  renewed effort and perseverance, 110–111
  respecting and accepting differences, 70–71
  sadness and hope, 100–101
  seeing with eyes of faith, 80–81
family, Christian, 43, 55–57
Fourth Gospel, 30
freedom, gift of, 94–95
free will, 43

G

Gabriel, angel, 125
Gifts of the Holy Spirit, 130–131, 142
Glory Prayer, 135
God
  attributes of, 40–42
  as Creator, 10–11, 17, 39–40, 53
  Law of, 23
  love of, for all people, 42
  as mystery, 14, 42, 49–52, 66
  presence of, 16, 25, 42

  quest for, 10
  revelation of, 13, 17, 20, 23, 42, 49
God the Father, 40, 51
God the Holy Spirit. See Holy Spirit.
God the Son. See Jesus Christ.
Good Friday, 88
Gospel, writing of, 29–31, 115
grace after meals, 137
grace before meals, 137
Great Commandment, 141

H-I

happiness, 9–10, 16, 106
heaven, 107
hell, 107
Holy Orders, sacrament of, 144
Holy Spirit, 123–132
  Advocate, 49, 104, 106, 125
  charisms of, 128
  Church's mission and, 127–128
  Gifts of, 130–131, 142
  as Giver of Life, 126
  grace of, 128
  as guide and helper, 42, 51, 104, 106, 111, 125–126
  Jesus and, 125–126
  in Old Testament, 124
  Pentecost and, 127
  present within us, 126
  promise of, 125
  sacraments and, 127, 130
  as source of unity, 127–128
  temples of, Christians as, 17, 126, 128, 130
  work of, 24–25, 34, 53–54, 64, 124–126
hope, 101, 106
Hosea the Prophet, 23
human beings, created in God's image, 43

image of God, humans as, 43
Immaculate Conception, 64
Incarnation, 66
initiation, Christian, 35
inspiration of the Bible, 20
intellect, 43
Isaiah the Prophet, 64, 84–85, 87
Israelites, 23, 41, 74

J

Jesus Christ
  appearances of, to disciples, 114–118
  baptism of, 68
  birth of, 63, 67
  Crucifixion of, 95–97
  as fulfillment of Law and Prophets, 64, 67, 78
  Incarnation, 66
  infancy and childhood of, 67
  at Last Supper, 51
  miracles, 31–32, 34
  Passion and death of, 78, 93–102
  public ministry of, 68
  Resurrection of, 101, 103–110
  as revelation of God, 23
  sacrifice of, 69, 85, 98

symbols for, 69
temptation of, in desert, 68
Transfiguration of, 73–82
true God and true man, 65–66
Jesus Christ, names and titles of:
Alpha and Omega, 69
Anointed One, 96
Bread of Life, 69
Christ, 75
Head of the Church, 127
Immanuel, 64
Lamb of God, 69
Light of World, 118
Lord, 33, 65, 115, 117–118, 120
Messiah, 30, 34, 75
New Adam, 44, 96
New Covenant, 22–23
Savior, 64, 67, 75, 120
Son of God, 30, 34, 51, 54, 63–72, 75, 78, 96
Son of Man, 33, 44
suffering Servant, 88
Word of God, 54, 65, 78
John the Baptist, 68, 127
John Paul II, Pope, 79, 99, 129
John XXIII, Blessed, 67
Julius II, Pope, 129

K-L-M
kingdom of God, 68, 98, 106, 108

Last Judgment, 108
Last Supper, 51
Law of God, Jesus as fulfillment of, 67, 78
lectio divina, 28
life after death, 107–108. See also eternal life.
light and darkness, symbols of, 118–119
literary genre, 21
Lord's Day, 105
Lord's Prayer, 135

Magnificat, 138
Mary
Annunciation, 125
Ever-Virgin, 64
Immaculate Conception, 64
as Mother of God, 64
as mother of Jesus, 64, 125
marriage, 43.
Matrimony, sacrament of, 144
Mass. See Eucharist.
Messiah, 30, 34, 75
miracle(s), 31–32, 34
missionary work of Church, 127–128
monotheism, 41
moral virtues, 142
Morning Prayer, 137
Moses, 23, 74–76, 78
Mother Teresa, Blessed of Calcutta, 79
mountains in Scripture, significance of, 74
mystery of God, 14, 42, 49–52, 66

N-O-P
New Adam, 96
New Covenant, 23
New Testament, 20–22
Nicaea, Council of First, 51–52, 66
Nicene Creed, 40, 136
Noah, 22

Old Testament, 20–22, 41
omnipresence, 42
oral tradition, 20
original justice, 44, 94
original sin, 44, 94
Our Father, 135

particular judgment, 107
Paschal Mystery, 78, 85–88, 93–102, 103–112, 103–110
Passion and death of Christ, 78, 93–102
Paul VI, Pope, 67
Penance, sacrament of. See Reconciliation, sacrament of.
Pentecost, 127
People of God, Church as, 127
Pharisees, 33–34
polytheism, 41
Pool of Siloam, 32
Pontius Pilate, 98, 105
pope, ministry of, 24, 127
prayer
being with God in, 16
lectio divina, 28
precepts of Church, 41
prophet(s), 83–85
Providence, divine 42
purgatory, 107

Q-R-S
Reconciliation, sacrament of, 144, 145
Redemption, 95
religious education, 15
Resurrection, 91, 95, 103–110
stories, 114–118
Revelation, divine, 13
reverence, gift of, 130–131
right judgment, gift of, 130–131
Rosary, 139

sacraments, 144
Sacraments of Healing, 144
Sacraments of Initiation, 142, 144
Sacraments at Service of Communion, 144
Sacred Scripture. See Bible.
Sacred Tradition, 24
sacrifice of Jesus Christ, 69, 88, 91, 95
saints,
Albert the Great, 12
Athanasius, 51
Augustine of Hippo, 10–11, 25, 128
Elizabeth Bayley Seton, 15
John the Apostle and Evangelist, 30–31
Leonard of Port Maurice, 99
Paul the Apostle, 14, 104, 128

Peter the Apostle, 75, 114, 116–117
Philip Neri, 109
Teresa of Avila, 41
Thomas the Apostle, 115
salvation, 22, 44, 50, 53–54, 75
sanctification, 53–54
Sarah, 23
secular humanism, 13
secularism, 13
Sermon on the Mount, 74
servant songs, 85–86
seven, symbolism of number, 118
Shroud of Turin, 97
Sign of the Cross, 35, 38, 135
signs and symbols of Christ, 69
sin(s)
redemption from, through Pascal Mystery, 95–96, 98. See also salvation.
Mary, free from, 64
original, 44, 94
Social Justice, Basic Principles of the Church's Teaching on, 143
Solomon, King, 23
soul, human, 43, 107–108
Spiritual Works of Mercy, 142
stained-glass windows, 119
Stations of the Cross, 99, 140
suffering, 78, 85–86, 88, 90–91, 95–96
suffering Servant, 83–92
Sunday, 105

T-U-V-W-X-Y-Z
Tabernacles, Feast of, 74
Temple in Jerusalem, 67
temples of Holy Spirit, Christians as, 17, 126, 128, 130
temptation, 22, 94
Ten Commandments, 74, 141
Teresa of Calcutta, Blessed Mother, 79
Tradition, Sacred, 24
Transfiguration of Jesus, 73–82
Trinity, 49–58, 104
truth
knowledge and understanding of, 12
God as, 42

understanding, gift of, 130–131
Ur, 21

Vatican Council II, 67
veneration of cross, 88, 102
vocation prayer, 137

wisdom, gift on, 130–131
wonder and awe, gift of, 130–131
word of God, see Bible
Word of God
Bible as, 17, 20, 26
Jesus as, 54, 65

YHWH, 65, 74–75

Zechariah, Canticle of, 72

Credits